Editor
Mary S. Jones, M.A.

Editor in Chief
Karen J. Goldfluss, M.S. Ed.

Cover Artist
Barb Lorseyedi

Imaging
James Edward Grace
Craig Gunnell

Publisher

Mary D. Smith, M.S. Ed.

W9-AUJ-560

TCR 2937

101 Activities for *Fast Finishers*

Grade 2

Keep kids engaged once their work is done!

Includes language arts, math, and critical thinking activities.

Great resource for busy teachers and quick-to-finish students!

Teacher Created Resources

Teacher Created Resources
6421 Industry Way
Westminster, CA 92683
www.teachercreated.com

ISBN: 978-1-4206-2937-8

© 2011 Teacher Created Resources
Made in U.S.A.

Teacher Created Resources

TABLE OF CONTENTS

INTRODUCTION

All students work at different speeds. Many take about the same amount of time to finish their work. Some are slower than others, and some are faster than others. You've probably been asked, "I'm done, what do I do now?" more times than you can count. But what's a teacher to do when one or more students finish early? The activity pages in *101 Activities for Fast Finishers* are the answer.

The 101 activities in this book focus on language arts, math, and critical thinking, and are divided as follows:

- Lively Language Arts (35 activities)
- Mind-Bender Math (35 activities)
- Beyond Brainy (31 activities)

Each activity has been labeled with an approximate amount of time that it will take students to complete. The estimated times range from 5 to 15 minutes. It is recommended that you copy, in advance, several pages representing the different times, and have them on hand to distribute, as needed. When a student asks you that famous "What do I do now?" question, a quick look at the clock will tell you which activity to give him or her. These activities will also be helpful to keep in your emergency substitute file as filler activities.

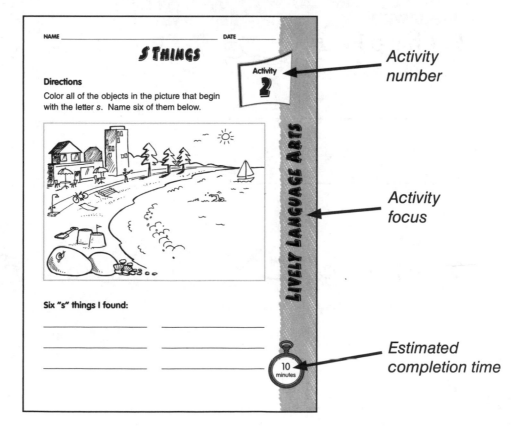

MIXED UP

Directions

Unscramble the letters to make the word that matches the picture. Then, make another word from the same letters.

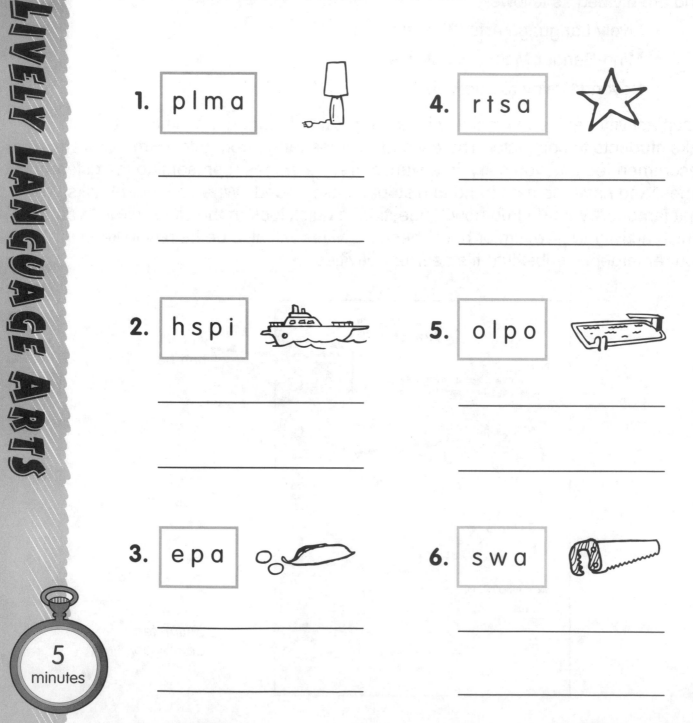

1. | p l m a |

_____

_____

4. | r t s a |

_____

_____

2. | h s p i |

_____

_____

5. | o l p o |

_____

_____

3. | e p a |

_____

_____

6. | s w a |

_____

_____

S THINGS

Directions

Color all of the objects in the picture that begin with the letter *s*. Name six of them below.

LIVELY LANGUAGE ARTS

Six "s" things I found:

_____   _____

_____   _____

_____   _____

10 minutes

BACK TO FRONT

Activity 3

Directions

Write each word backwards on the line and draw a picture of the new word in the box. For example: pat = tap.

LIVELY LANGUAGE ARTS

1. ten = _____

5. nip = _____

2. god = _____

6. tops = _____

3. tar = _____

7. pets = _____

4. but = _____

8. reed = _____

5 minutes

CHANGING LETTERS

Directions

Change the **last** letter in each word to make a new word that matches the picture.

1. crowd

_____

2. food

_____

3. mood

_____

4. sheen

_____

5. bald

_____

6. wool

_____

7. wing

_____

8. carp

_____

LIVELY LANGUAGE ARTS

5 minutes

How Many?

LIVELY LANGUAGE ARTS

Directions

Color **red** those boxes that contain the names of things that have **four legs**.

Color **yellow** those boxes that contain the names of things that have only **two legs**.

chair	girl	pig	goat
boy	dog	goose	lady
hen	owl	tiger	zebra
cat	duck	man	table

5 minutes

LITTLE WORDS

Directions

Find a little word in each of the big words and write it on the line at the bottom of the box. Then draw pictures of what you have found. The first one has been done for you.

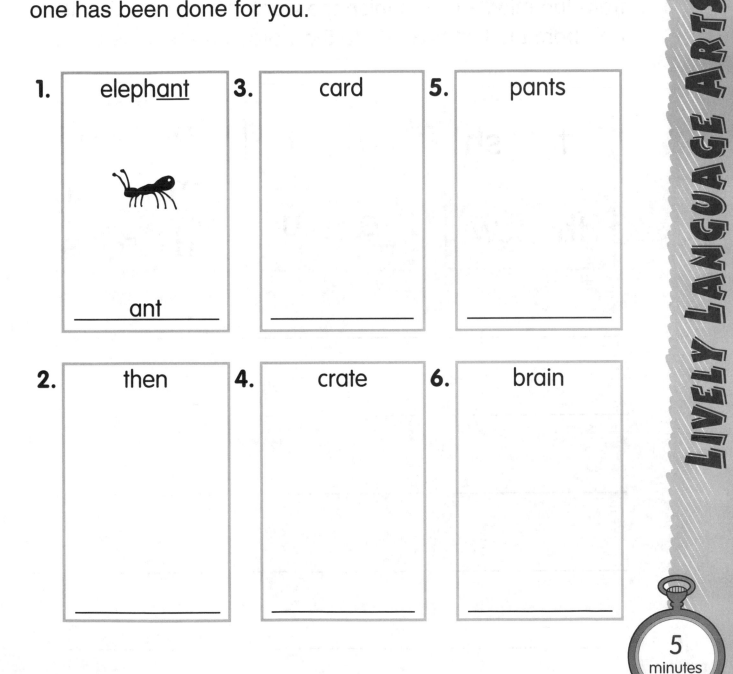

1. eleph<u>ant</u>

_____ant_____

3. card

_____

5. pants

_____

2. then

_____

4. crate

_____

6. brain

_____

LIVELY LANGUAGE ARTS

5 minutes

BOX ON

Directions

How many words can you make using the letters in the boxes? Start with a letter or letter pair from the first box on the left. Then use a letter from the middle box. Finish the word with a letter or letter pair from the last box. Write the words on the lines below.

CROSSWORDS

Activity
8

Directions

Use the picture clues across and down to complete the crosswords.

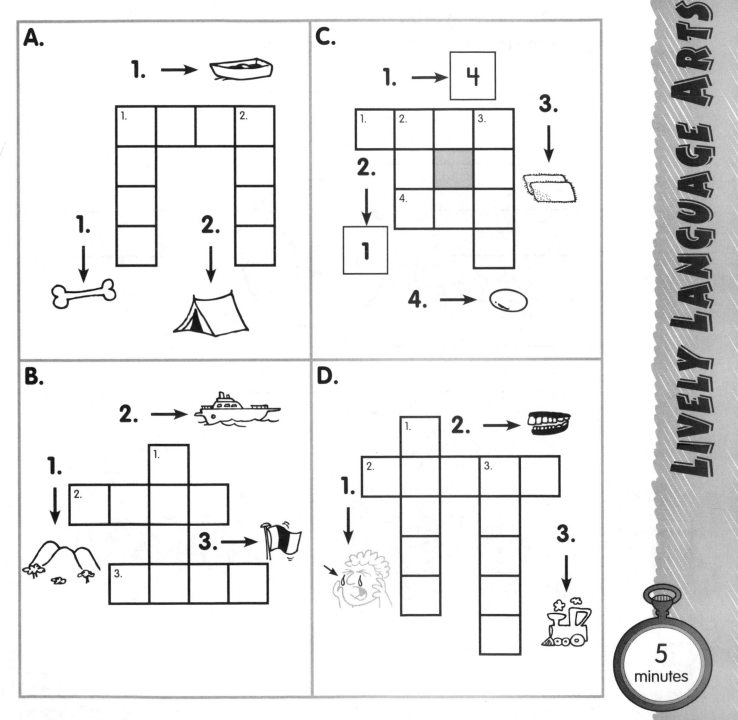

WORD MAKE

Activity
9

Directions

How many new words can you make by adding a letter or letters to the word *at*? You can add letters to the beginning or the end, or both. Write as many words as you can on the lines below. Then draw pictures of two of them in the box.

at

LIVELY LANGUAGE ARTS

10 minutes

DRAWING IN

Activity
10

Directions

Look at the picture, and then follow the directions below.

1. Draw a bird in the cage.

2. Draw three fish in the fish bowl.

3. Draw a chair at the table.

4. Draw a cat sleeping under the fish bowl.

5. Draw a clock on the wall.

LIVELY LANGUAGE ARTS

5 minutes

FIND MY NAME

LIVELY LANGUAGE ARTS

Directions

Read each set of clues to find out the name of each object. Write its name on the line and draw it in the box.

1. What am I?

- My first letter is in *cap* but not in *cat*.

- My second letter is in *dig* but not in *dug*.

- My third letter is in *log* but not in *lot*.

I am a _____.

Draw me!

2. What am I?

- My first letter is in *jab* but not in *jam*.

- My second letter is in *net* but not in *nut*.

- My third letter is in *den* but not in *hen*.

I am a _____.

Draw me!

5 minutes

SORTING

Activity
12

Directions

Write the words in the box under the correct headings below.

cake	socks	games	pizza
shoes	eggs	fruit	sweater
tennis	cards	hat	football

Things to Eat   **Things to Play**   **Things to Wear**

_____   _____   _____

_____   _____   _____

_____   _____   _____

_____   _____   _____

5 minutes

LIVELY LANGUAGE ARTS

WHAT'S THERE?

Activity
13

Directions

Look at the picture. Color the boxes below that contain the names of things in the picture. Then write a sentence about the picture.

car	tree	bus	sails	book
cow	fence	chair	snake	tent
elephant	house	boat	table	plate
ball	fire	cup	water	rocks

10
minutes

_____

_____

_____

RHYMING WORDS

Directions

Words with the same ending sound are rhyming words. Circle the words that rhyme in each row.

1.	car	star	stir	scar
2.	fancy	Nancy	antsy	pants
3.	solar	parlor	polar	molar
4.	hairy	hurry	fairy	Jerry
5.	calf	laugh	ruff	half
6.	head	sad	bed	fed
7.	back	cake	rake	shake
8.	pipe	dip	stripe	type

LIVELY LANGUAGE ARTS

For each word, write three more rhyming words.

9. look: _____ , _____ , _____

10. tie: _____ , _____ , _____

11. hug: _____ , _____ , _____

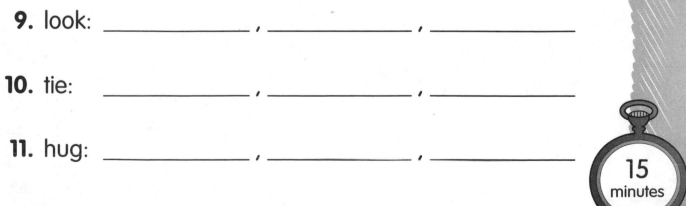

15 minutes

Nursery Rhyme Time

LIVELY LANGUAGE ARTS

Directions

Draw lines to connect the parts of these nursery rhymes. Then draw a picture of one of the rhymes in the space below.

Jack and Jill	runs through the town
Rub-a-dub-dub	three men in a tub
Wee Willie Winkie	sat on a wall
Little Boy Blue	come blow your horn
Humpty Dumpty	went up the hill
Little Bo Peep	has lost her sheep

10 minutes

KNOWING NOUNS

Activity
16

Directions

A noun is the name of a person, place, or thing.
Color each noun that is a **person red**.
Color each noun that is a **place yellow**.
Color each noun that is a **thing blue**.

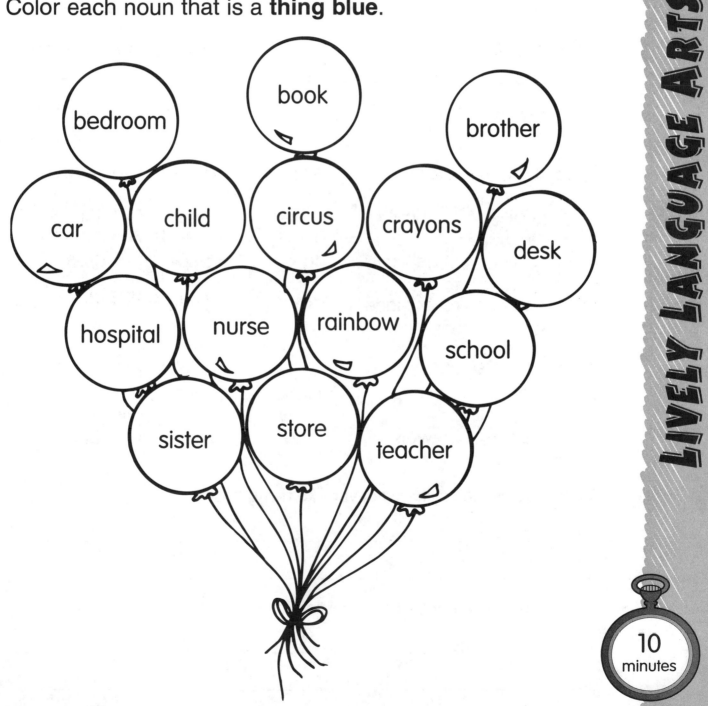

LIVELY LANGUAGE ARTS

10 minutes

WACKY VERBS

Activity
17

LIVELY LANGUAGE ARTS

Directions

Verbs are action words. Color **red** the boxes that are verbs that only people do. Color **blue** the verbs that only animals do. If the verb is something that both people and animals do, color the box **green**.

quack	skip	fly	run	jump
grow	cook	turn	roll	push
swim	ski	sing	drive	bark
eat	shoot	scratch	hiss	bite
play	gallop	talk	whisper	drink
skate	roller blade	sit	speak	yell
gulp	hop	trot	throw	dress
fall	chirp	whistle	swallow	lay
sleep	walk	read	write	think

Write a sentence saying what you like doing best of all.

I like _____

_____

Write a sentence about the interesting things you have seen animals do.

I have seen animals _____

_____

15
minutes

WHICH ADJECTIVE?

Activity

18

Directions

An adjective is a word that describes something. Read each adjective phrase in the box. Decide whether each adjective tells how many, what kind, or which one. Rewrite the phrases in the correct columns.

six boys	short hair	million dollars	one teacher
these books	rich man	that bus	green shoes
a dozen eggs	hot cement	this computer	any class

How Many?	What Kind?	Which One?

LIVELY LANGUAGE ARTS

10 minutes

DESCRIBING OBJECTS

Activity
19

Directions

Write a word from the box that matches the description in each sentence.

apple pie	fire	shoes	sky
bed	kitten	skateboard	tree

1. The tall, green, leafy _____ was swaying in the wind.

2. The furry, black _____ curled up in the sunshine and slept.

3. I love to eat spicy, warm, delicious, homemade _____.

4. My _____ goes clickety-clack as I roll down the street.

5. The big, soft, comfy _____ looked great when I was sleepy.

6. These old, dirty, worn-out _____ need to be thrown away.

7. The warm, crackling _____ feels good on a cool night.

8. The beautiful, blue _____ stretched above us.

PICTURE THIS

Directions

Look at the picture, and then read the sentences below. After each, write *yes* or *no*.

1. The man is cooking. _____

2. A girl is sweeping the floor. _____

3. A dog is drinking some milk. _____

4. There are two birds in the cage. _____

5. A girl is setting the table. _____

6. A pot on the stove is boiling. _____

LIVELY LANGUAGE ARTS

5 minutes

COMPOUND WORDS

Activity
21

Directions

Combining two words into one unique word makes a compound word. The meaning of the compound word can be determined by looking at its two word parts. Circle the eight words in the box that are compound words. Then write four sentences using one of the compound words in each one.

baggage	jacket	raincoat	tooth
bathrobe	lips	shoelace	turtleneck
bracelet	necklace	stocking	under
fingers	overalls	sweater	uniform
glasses	pajamas	swimsuit	wristwatch

1. _____

_____

2. _____

_____

3. _____

_____

4. _____

_____

15
minutes

PARTS OF SOMETHING

Activity

22

Directions

Each set of words below is part of something larger. In the boxes, draw what you think each thing is.

1. floor　　　　door 　ceiling　　　wall	**3.** handlebars　spokes 　　wheels　　　pedals
2. leaves　　　bark 　branches　　roots	**4.** feathers　　　tail 　　wings　　　beak

LIVELY LANGUAGE ARTS

10 minutes

RHYME TIME

Directions

Use the words in the boxes to complete each nursery rhyme.

crown   after   water   hill

Jack and Jill went up the _____
1

To fetch a pail of _____
2

Jack fell down and broke his _____
3

And Jill came tumbling _____ .
4

snow   go   went   lamb

Mary had a little _____
5

Its fleece was white as _____
6

And everywhere that Mary _____
7

The lamb was sure to _____ .
8

Lively Language Arts

5 minutes

ABC ORDER

Activity 24

Directions

Write each list of words in alphabetical order.

List A
candy
cake
chocolate
cookies
caramel

List B
puppy
penguin
pelican
parrot
panther

List C
Alicia
Alex
Ann
Allison
Amanda

LIVELY LANGUAGE ARTS

List A

1. _____

2. _____

3. _____

4. _____

5. _____

List B

1. _____

2. _____

3. _____

4. _____

5. _____

List C

1. _____

2. _____

3. _____

4. _____

5. _____

10 minutes

SIMILES

Activity
25

Directions

Choose the best word from the box to complete each simile.

mouse	ghost
ox	wink
night	snail
kitten	whip
fox	bird

1. As white as a _____

2. As strong as an _____

3. As quiet as a _____

4. As free as a _____

5. As quick as a _____

6. As sly as a _____

7. As black as _____

8. As smart as a _____

9. As slow as a _____

10. As playful as a _____

5 minutes

LIVELY LANGUAGE ARTS

MULTIPLE MEANINGS

Directions

Some words have more than one meaning.
Match each **bold** word to its two meanings.

to fasten items together	**box**	the cresting water in the ocean
to play a sport with balls and pins	**bowl**	twelve inches in length
a student	**can**	a corn cob
a light rain	**ear**	a metal or aluminum container
a cube-shaped container	**foot**	an item worn around a man's neck
metal to fasten papers together	**pupil**	to play a sport that allows hitting
moving a hand back and forth	**shower**	a standard food item
to be able to	**staple**	a round, deep dish
a lower body part	**tie**	used to clean oneself
something to hear with	**wave**	the inner part of one's eye

LIVELY LANGUAGE ARTS

15 minutes

WORD PICTURES

Directions

Complete the story using words instead of pictures.

One day a _____ was swimming in the

_____ when it saw a _____

and a _____ playing on the bank.

The _____ had built its _____

nearby. In the _____ , it had laid

three _____ . Just then, a _____

crawled out of a _____ in the ground

and so the _____ flew away.

5
minutes

WHICH WORD?

Directions

Read the sentences below. Color the box with the correct word to complete each sentence.

1. I picked the | lamb | lemon | lamp | that was growing on the tree.

2. We can get | oil | grass | wool | from a sheep.

3. There are lots of flowers growing in the | garden | goose | mail |.

4. If you were writing a story, you would use a | jelly | pencil | dog |.

5. At the zoo, I saw a | poor | tiger | giant |.

6. You can carry water in a | bucket | fig | pony |.

LIVELY LANGUAGE ARTS

5 minutes

TEETER-TOTTER WORDS

LIVELY LANGUAGE ARTS

Directions

Antonyms are words that are opposite in meaning. On a teeter-totter, when one side is up, the other side is down. *Up* and *down* are antonyms. Read the word on one end of the teeter-totter. Write an antonym for each word on the other end.

1. night
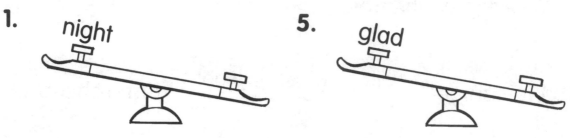

5. glad

2. light

6. hard
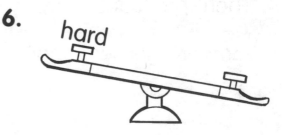

3. hot

7. good

4. ugly
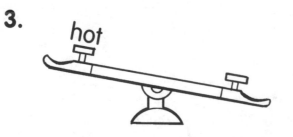

8. bottom
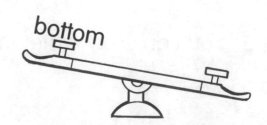

⏱ 10 minutes

HOMOPHONES

Activity
30

Directions

Homophones are words that sound the same but are spelled differently and have different meanings. Draw a line connecting each homophone to its right meaning.

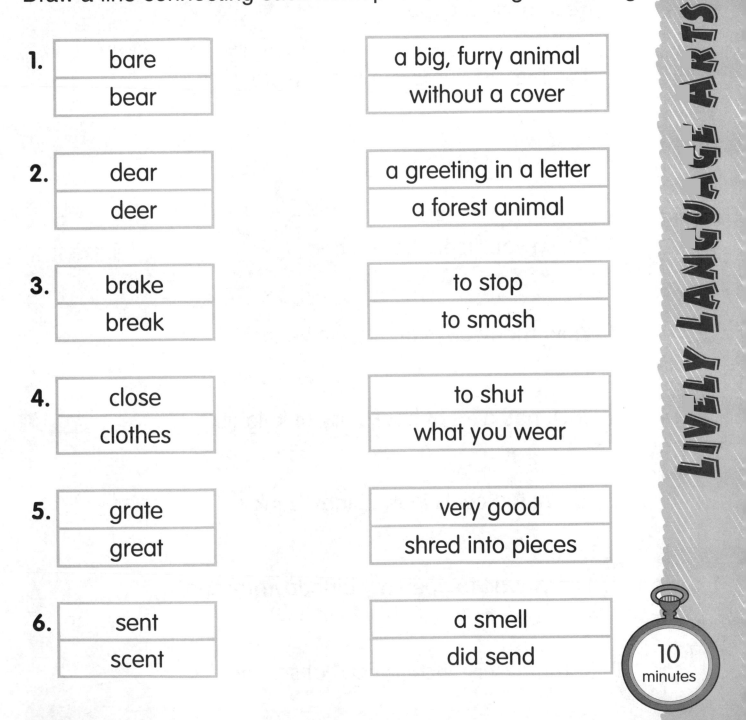

1. | bare |
   | bear |

   | a big, furry animal |
   | without a cover |

2. | dear |
   | deer |

   | a greeting in a letter |
   | a forest animal |

3. | brake |
   | break |

   | to stop |
   | to smash |

4. | close |
   | clothes |

   | to shut |
   | what you wear |

5. | grate |
   | great |

   | very good |
   | shred into pieces |

6. | sent |
   | scent |

   | a smell |
   | did send |

10 minutes

LIVELY LANGUAGE ARTS

ENDING MARKS

Directions

Read each sentence. Decide if a period (.), a question mark (?), or an exclamation point (!) is needed at the end. Write the correct mark in the box.

1. Did that fish jump out of the water

2. Ouch, that hurt my leg

3. Brush your teeth before bed

4. How many days are in two years

5. Jack has a lot of books about knights

6. Count the coins in the piggy bank

7. I can't wait to open my birthday presents

8. Tomorrow is "Picture Day" at school

10 minutes

It's a Sentence!

Activity
32

Directions

Rewrite the sentences below. Be sure to begin each one with a capital letter. Add correct ending punctuation to each sentence.

1. is today your birthday

_____

2. a party is a wonderful idea

_____

3. mike will bring the birthday cake

_____

4. how many candles will be on the cake

_____

5. will there be a clown

_____

6. we can help you decorate

_____

7. karen will bring the balloons

_____

8. the party will have lots of music

_____

9. there will be many presents

_____

10. what a wonderful birthday it will be

_____

LIVELY LANGUAGE ARTS

15 minutes

HIDDEN MEANING

Directions

Read each short story. Circle the best answer for each question.

1. Bob wears a wig. He puts on big shoes and silly clothes. Bob paints his face with makeup. Then, he goes to work. What is Bob's job?

   fireman   clown   bus driver

2. Sue could hear meowing. She walked over to the tree and looked up. What was in the tree?

   a bird   a dog   a cat

3. Mom did not want to cook dinner. The doorbell rang. A man was standing there with a thin, square box. What was for dinner?

   pizza   an apple   cereal

4. Mark drew a shape on his paper. He did not lift his pencil at all. The shape had no straight lines. What shape did Mark draw?

   square   circle   triangle

ELEPHANT KING

Directions

Write a strange story to share with your friends.
Fill in the blanks below, but do not look ahead at
the story. Then use the words to complete your strange tale.

1. color _____
2. boy's name _____
3. body part _____
4. place _____
5. action _____
6. old vehicle _____
7. fruit (plural) _____

8. food (plural) _____
9. candy (plural) _____
10. favorite food _____
11. candy bar (plural) _____
12. body part _____
13. fruit _____

LIVELY LANGUAGE ARTS

A large, _____ coconut fell off the tree and hit

_____ , the Elephant King, right on the
    2

_____ . He was on his way to the
    3

_____ to _____ . His servants
    4   5

stopped their _____ and ran to see if he was feeling
    6

alright. The king started to talk really strangely. " _____
                                       7

and _____ , _____ , and
    8   9

_____ !" he said. "King, whatever is the matter?"
    10

they all asked at once. He screamed, "Jumping _____ ,
                                            11

my _____ hurts!" The nurse gave him a shot of
    12

_____ juice. He jumped off the table and was
    13

never heard from again!

15
minutes

MONSTER MEETS ANT

Activity
35

Directions

Write a strange story to share with your friends. Fill in the blanks below, but do not look ahead at the story. Then use the words to complete your strange tale.

LIVELY LANGUAGE ARTS

1. flying animal _____
2. weekday _____
3. building material _____
4. color _____
5. color _____
6. sound (add -ing) _____

7. kind word _____
8. verb (add -ed) _____
9. size word _____
10. light fixture (plural) _____
11. place _____
12. thing (plural) _____

A brilliant orange _____ flew over the castle one summer
                          1

_____ night. Sir Monster Knight rode up to the _____
   2   3

castle on his new, flaming _____ horse. His armor was shiny
                                4

and made of strong metal. A window was open in the far tower.

A maiden with _____ hair was looking out the window,
                    5

waiting for the knight to come. The horse made a loud "_____"
                                                              6

sound. Sir Knight rode below her window and softly whispered

"_____" to her. The princess _____ down a silk
     7   8

rope and climbed onto the back of his _____ horse. All the
                                            9

_____ in the castle went on, but the princess rode off into the
   10

night with Sir Knight in shining armor to _____ . The two rode
                                               11

_____ for hours and lived happily ever after!
   12

15 minutes

WHOSE BALLOONS?

Directions

Toni, Sally, and Mika bought some balloons but they became mixed up.

- Toni's balloons have even numbers less than 20.
- Sally's balloons have odd numbers less than 20.
- Mika's balloons all have numbers more than 20.

Color Toni's balloons **red**, Sally's **yellow**, and Mika's **blue**.

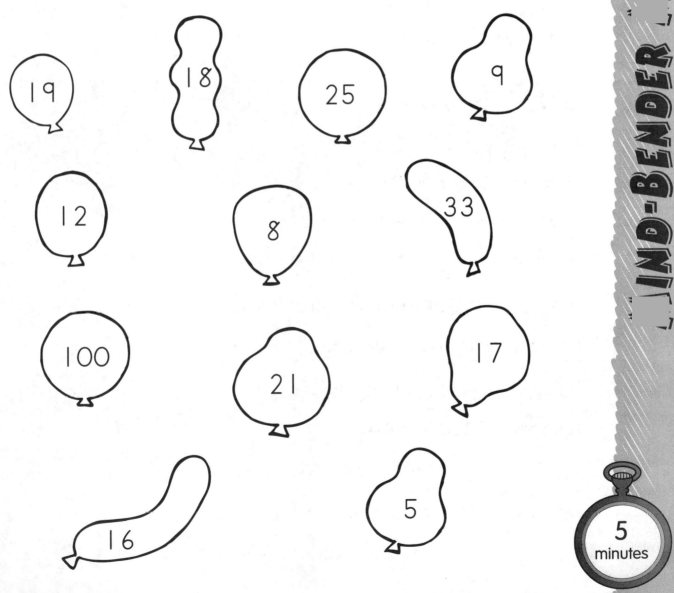

PATHWAYS

Directions

Color **red** the 2s path through the grid to reach 48. To do this, keep counting by 2. All the colored boxes must be touching, either at the side, top, bottom, or corner. Now color **blue** the 3s path to 48. To do this, keep counting by 3.

2s path ↓   3s path ↓

8	3	2	0	4	8	40	3	99	21
5	9	7	4	11	48	21	6	8	14
11	12	13	6	46	9	12	9	7	11
3	6	41	8	44	7	15	3	6	9
7	9	10	21	16	42	18	21	9	8
16	14	12	22	13	40	7	24	27	48
18	12	11	23	36	38	6	7	30	45
20	13	20	5	34	6	5	9	33	42
14	22	24	7	32	5	8	8	36	39
15	18	26	28	30	4	3	11	6	7
16	17	19	9	11	0	11	4	5	6

10 minutes

40

NUMBER SENTENCES

Directions

How many number sentences can you make to equal 8? Use the numbers in the boxes and the signs +, −, and x. Write your number sentences on the lines below. One has been done for you.

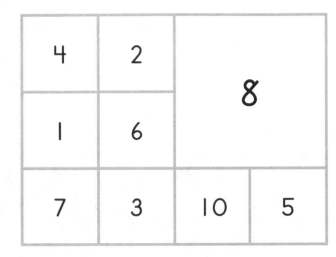

4	2	
1	6	8
7	3	10	5

MIND-BENDER MAT

6 + 2 = 8

_____   _____

_____   _____

_____   _____

_____   _____

5 minutes

SAME ANSWERS

Activity
39

Directions

Solve the number sentences below. The same answer will appear at least three times. Color each group of rectangles with the same answer in the same color. You will need eight different colors.

5 + 5 =	3 x 3 =	4 x 2 =	8 + 2 =	12 − 3 =
4 x 5 =	10 + 2 =	2 x 2 =	10 + 4 =	9 + 3 =
10 − 4 =	8 − 4 =	10 + 10 =	12 − 6 =	10 − 2 =
5 + 4 =	13 − 4 =	6 + 6 =	2 x 10 =	2 x 7 =
6 + 2 =	6 + 4 =	10 − 6 =	4 + 2 =	13 + 1 =

One of the answers appears four times.

It is the number _____ .

10 minutes

TRIANGLE SEARCH

Directions

Look closely at the picture. Count all the triangles.
Then draw a picture in the box using mostly
triangles.

There are _____ triangles.

5
minutes

WHICH PUPPIES?

Activity 41

Directions

The mother dog has just had six puppies. All of her puppies have even numbers and are less than 25. Color in only the puppies that belong to the mother dog.

Challenge

List all even numbers between 1 and 25.

_____

_____

NAME ______________________________ DATE ______________

Count the Shapes

Activity 42

Directions

Use the shapes below to help you gather information for the graph. Color in the graph to show the number of each shape shown. Then write in the shape that is found most often.

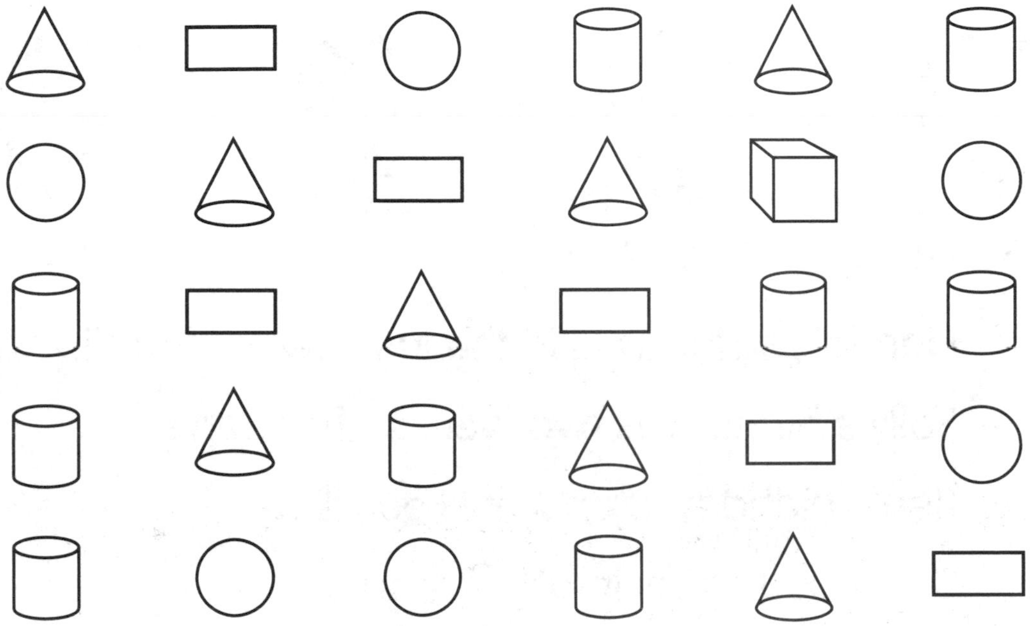

cone	cube	circle	cylinder	rectangle

The shape found most often is the ____________________ .

MIND-BENDER MATH

10 minutes

BIRTHDAYS

Directions

Hamid, Sally, Ben, and Jacinta all have their birthdays in April. Read all the clues, and then write each name next to the correct date.

Hamid   Sally   Ben   Jacinta

- Hamid's birthday is in the last week of April.
- Sally's birthday is two weeks after Ben's.
- Ben's birthday is on April Fools Day.
- 5 + 4 equals Jacinta's birthday.

1. _____ = April 1

2. _____ = April 9

3. _____ = April 16

4. _____ = April 28

5
minutes

KITES

Directions

Draw a line from each kite to the person with the correct answer. How many kites does each person have?

Activity 44

$7 + 2$	$6 + 4$	$6 + 6$	$5 + 4$	5×2
$6 + 3$	$5 + 5$	3×3	$8 + 4$	$12 - 2$
10×2	$10 + 2$	$10 + 10$	$18 + 2$	

| 12 | 9 | 20 | 10 |
| Zoe has ____ kites. | Jodi has ____ kites. | Tim has ____ kites. | Meg has ____ kites. |

10 minutes

COLOR BY NUMBER

Directions

Solve the number sentences in the picture to find out what color to use for each shape. Now color the picture using the color code.

8 = orange	15 = green
12 = blue	16 = brown
13 = purple	20 = yellow

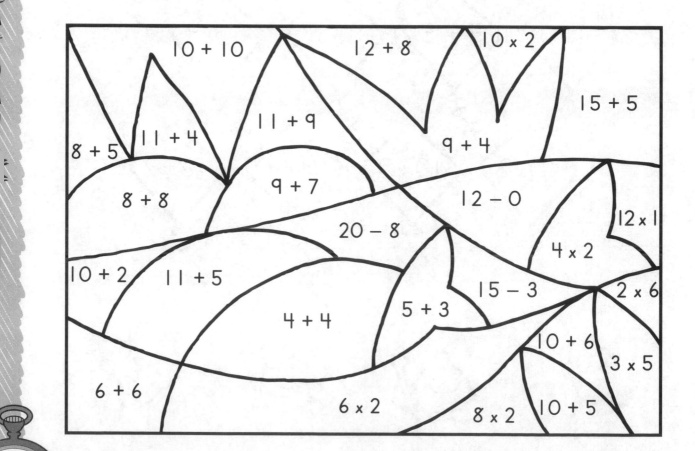

10 minutes

NUMBER MAZE

Activity
46

Directions

Solve the number sentences below.

1. 3 + 3 = _____   **5.** 5 + 5 = _____

2. 3 + 2 = _____   **6.** 7 + 7 = _____

3. 4 + 4 = _____   **7.** 6 + 5 = _____

4. 6 + 3 = _____

Now follow the answers to these sums to get through the maze, starting with the answer to number 1. As you go from number to number, you will pass through a letter. Write the letters in the boxes below to make the name of something you might use at school or home.

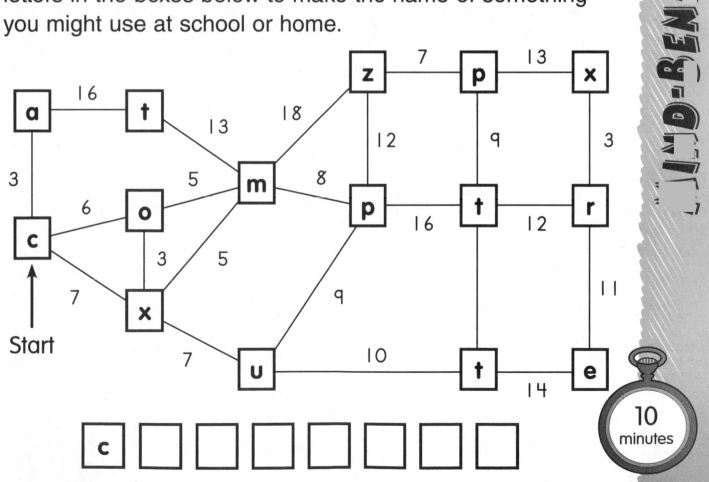

ANSWER BOX

Activity
47

Directions

Solve each number sentence. Then find the answer in the grid and color it as instructed.

1. 3 + 3 + 6 = _____ = brown

2. 7 – 3 – 3 = _____ = red

3. (5 × 2) + 6 = _____ = yellow

4. 10 + 10 = _____ = green

5. 4 + 5 + 6 = _____ = blue

6. (2 × 3) + 8 = _____ = orange

20	4	11	5	3
8	7	13	12	6
18	16	15	14	10
1	2	30	100	50

MIND-BENDER MATH

10 minutes

ANSWER MATCH

Activity
48

Directions

Look at the left and right sides in the columns below. On each side, there are equations that have the same answer. Draw lines between equations that have the same answer. The first one has been done for you.

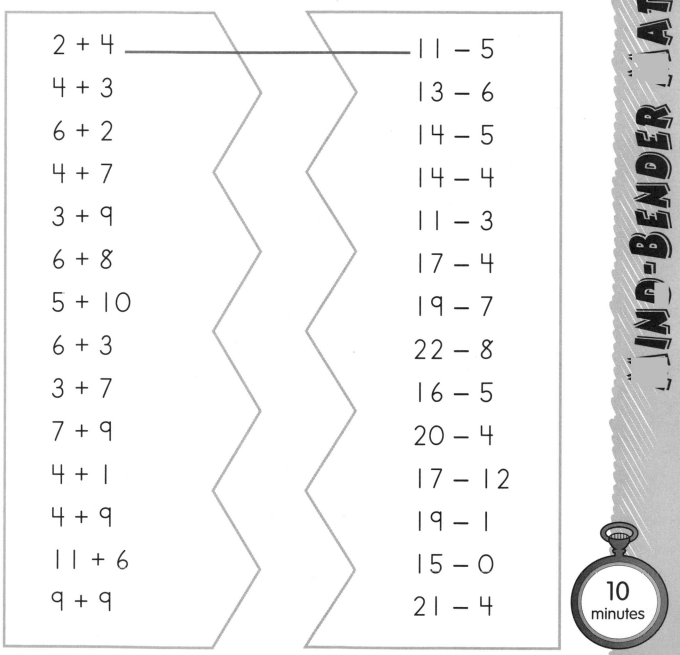

2 + 4	11 – 5
4 + 3	13 – 6
6 + 2	14 – 5
4 + 7	14 – 4
3 + 9	11 – 3
6 + 8	17 – 4
5 + 10	19 – 7
6 + 3	22 – 8
3 + 7	16 – 5
7 + 9	20 – 4
4 + 1	17 – 12
4 + 9	19 – 1
11 + 6	15 – 0
9 + 9	21 – 4

MIND-BENDER MAT

10 minutes

STANDARD FORM

Activity 49

Directions

Rewrite each number in standard form.

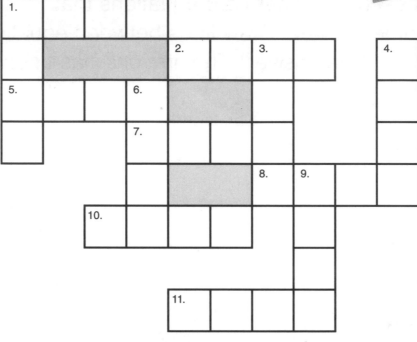

Across	Down
1. 4 thousands + 9 hundreds + 5 tens + 8 ones	**1.** 4 thousands + 1 hundred + 3 tens + 4 ones
2. 7 thousands + 3 hundreds + 5 tens + 2 ones	**3.** 5 thousands + 8 hundreds + 6 tens + 5 ones
5. 3 thousands + 8 hundreds + 3 tens + 9 ones	**4.** 7 thousands + 6 hundreds + 4 tens + 7 ones
7. 8 thousands + 7 hundreds + 8 tens + 6 ones	**6.** 9 thousands + 8 hundreds + 1 ten + 0 ones
8. 5 thousands + 1 hundred + 8 tens + 7 ones	**9.** 1 thousand + 2 hundreds + 5 tens + 1 one
10. 4 thousands + 0 hundreds + 1 ten + 8 ones	
11. 7 thousands + 9 hundreds + 5 tens + 1 one	

FLOWER ARRANGEMENTS

Directions

Draw lines between the flowers and the vases that belong together. Each vase has two flowers.

MIND-BENDER MATH

RIGHT ON TARGET

Activity
51

Directions

Find the sums of the numbers on the target. Where did Aaron's arrow land if he hit 60? Color that ring green.

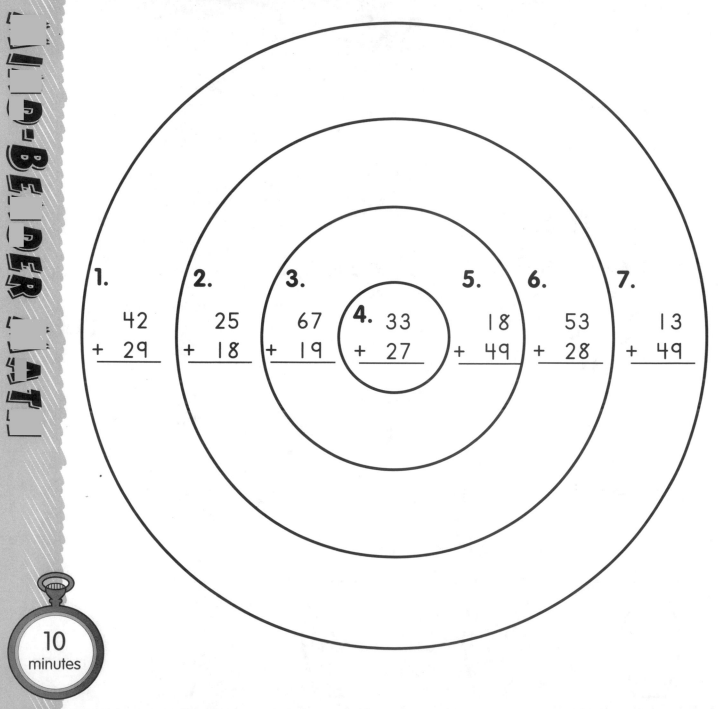

1.
$$42$$
$$+\ 29$$

2.
$$25$$
$$+\ 18$$

3.
$$67$$
$$+\ 19$$

4.
$$33$$
$$+\ 27$$

5.
$$18$$
$$+\ 49$$

6.
$$53$$
$$+\ 28$$

7.
$$13$$
$$+\ 49$$

10 minutes

TWELVES

Directions

Each math problem has a letter above it. In the empty squares below, write all the letters that appear above math problems that equal 12. Go from left to right. If you do it correctly, you will discover the name of a fruit.

o	t	r	a	b	n	g	p	e
6 + 6	3 + 4	6 x 2	3 x 4	10 – 7	8 + 4	7 + 5	10 + 10	9 + 3

The first letter has been put in for you.

o					

Draw the fruit.

COLOR CODE

Activity
53

Directions

Solve the number sentences in the rectangles. Then use the color code below to color the rectangles in the correct color.

10 = blue	12 = green	15 = red
16 = yellow	20 = pink	30 = orange

1. $(2 \times 6) + 3 =$	**6.** $(2 \times 4) + 2 =$	**11.** $(5 \times 4) - 5 =$
2. $(10 \times 3) - 10 =$	**7.** $20 - 2 - 2 =$	**12.** $3 + 9 + 4 + 4 =$
3. $20 - 10 =$	**8.** $(2 \times 6) + 8 =$	**13.** $(2 \times 4) + 4 =$
4. $7 + 4 + 5 =$	**9.** $2 \times 6 - 0 =$	**14.** $7 + 3 + 5 =$
5. $(5 \times 3) + 5 =$	**10.** $(2 \times 8) - 6 =$	**15.** $(5 \times 2) + 20 =$

15 minutes

MIND-BENDER MATH

FAVORITE SUBJECTS

Directions

Read the tally chart, and then answer the questions below.

Our Favorite Subjects	
Subject	**Tally of Votes**
math	|||
art	||||
history	|
science	卌
music	||
reading	卌 |
writing	|||
P.E.	卌
health	|

1. What subject is liked the most?_____

2. How many people liked it the most? _____

3. What subjects tied for second place?_____

4. Which subject tied with writing? _____

5. How many more liked math than history?_____

5 minutes

SQUARE UP

Activity

55

Directions

Count the number of squares. Write your answer below.

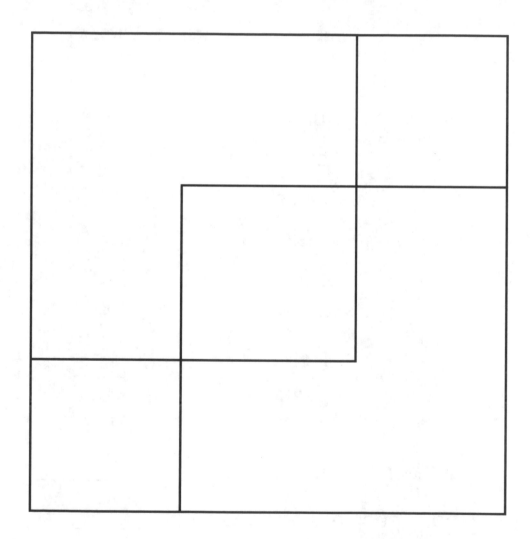

There are _____ squares.

Even Follows

Activity

56

Directions

On the puzzle below, follow only the lines with even numbers on them. As you follow these lines, you will pass through letters. Write these letters in the boxes below and you will discover the name of an animal. The first letter has been put in for you.

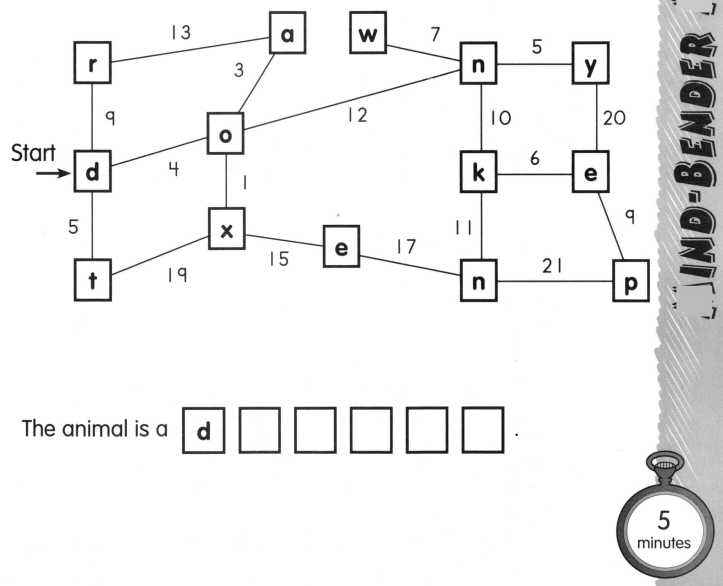

The animal is a | d | | | | | | .

MISSING NUMBERS

Activity
57

Directions

Look at the number pattern in each square. One number is missing. Write the missing number in each square.

1.

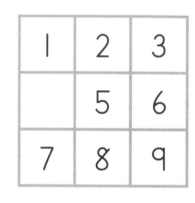

1	2	3
	5	6
7	8	9

4.

20	18	16
14		10
8	6	4

2.

5	10	15
20	25	
35	40	45

5.

2	4	6
8	10	
14	16	18

3.

1	3	5
7		11
13	15	17

6.

1	4	7
10	13	16
19	22	

WHAT'S IN THE BOX?

Activity
58

Directions

Find the sums. Then write the letter in each box that matches each sum. Read the word you spell and draw it in the box.

80	81	82	83	84	85	86	87
d	e	a	o	c	r	l	i

$$\begin{array}{r} 45 \\ +37 \\ \hline 82 \end{array}$$
a

$$\begin{array}{r} 24 \\ +60 \\ \hline \end{array}$$

$$\begin{array}{r} 62 \\ +23 \\ \hline \end{array}$$

$$\begin{array}{r} 58 \\ +25 \\ \hline \end{array}$$

$$\begin{array}{r} 12 \\ +72 \\ \hline \end{array}$$

$$\begin{array}{r} 36 \\ +47 \\ \hline \end{array}$$

$$\begin{array}{r} 40 \\ +40 \\ \hline \end{array}$$

$$\begin{array}{r} 52 \\ +35 \\ \hline \end{array}$$

$$\begin{array}{r} 32 \\ +54 \\ \hline \end{array}$$

$$\begin{array}{r} 48 \\ +33 \\ \hline \end{array}$$

5 minutes

BREAKFAST LINKS

Directions

There are two sausages and one egg for each child. Draw lines linking the sausages and egg to the child that has the correct answer on his or her plate. Use a different color for each line. One has been done for you.

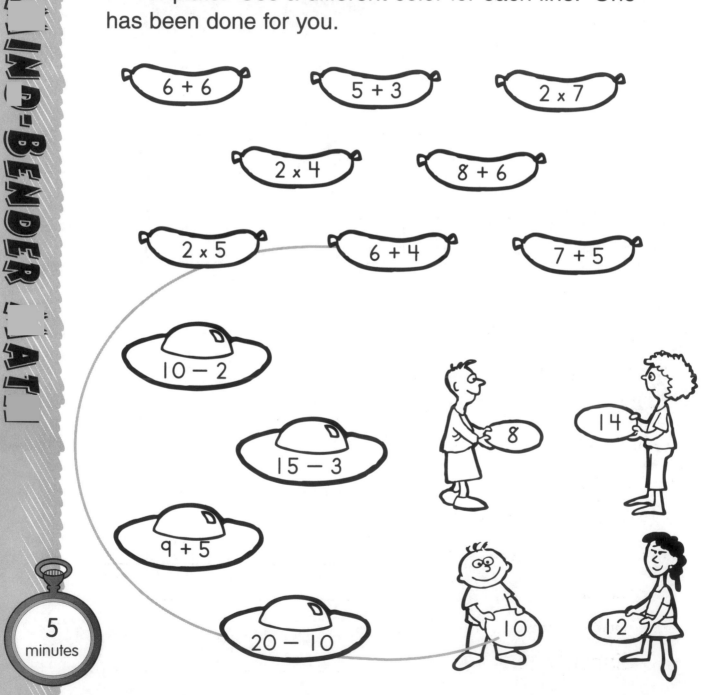

How Far?

Activity
60

Directions

Find the number of miles between the cities going through the fewest cities.

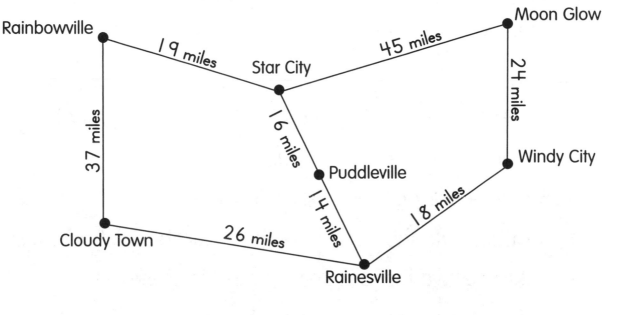

Ex: Rainbowville to Moon Glow _____ 19 + 45 = 64 miles

1. Rainbowville to Puddleville _____

2. Star City to Cloudy Town _____

3. Moon Glow to Rainbowville _____

4. Cloudy Town to Puddleville _____

5. Rainbowville to Rainesville _____

6. Moon Glow to Puddleville _____

7. Star City to Windy City _____

8. Cloudy Town to Windy City _____

9. Rainesville to Moon Glow _____

15 minutes

IT'S BANANAS!

Directions

Our class held a banana-eating contest last week. Using the numbers in the box and the clues below, can you figure out how many bananas each person ate? Write your answers in the chart below.

14   6   8   10   12

- Janet ate the most bananas.

- Sula ate the least number of bananas.

- Matthew ate the second highest number of bananas.

- Mike ate two bananas less than Matthew.

- Paul ate two more bananas than Sula.

Name	Bananas
Matthew	
Paul	
Janet	
Sula	
Mike	

5 minutes

MIND-BENDER MAT

BOUNCING BALLS

Activity

62

Directions

Compare the numbers on the basketballs using the symbols <, >, or =. Draw them on each ball.

Remember…

< means "less than"   > means "greater than"   = means "equal to"

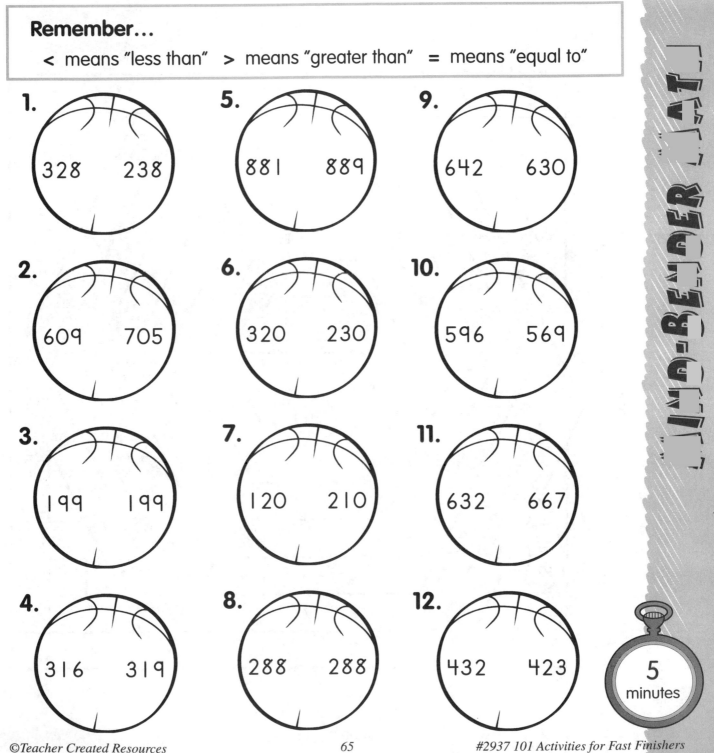

1. 328   238

2. 609   705

3. 199   199

4. 316   319

5. 881   889

6. 320   230

7. 120   210

8. 288   288

9. 642   630

10. 596   569

11. 632   667

12. 432   423

5 minutes

EVEN NUMBERS

Activity 63

Directions

Follow the path of even numbers to reach the end of the maze.

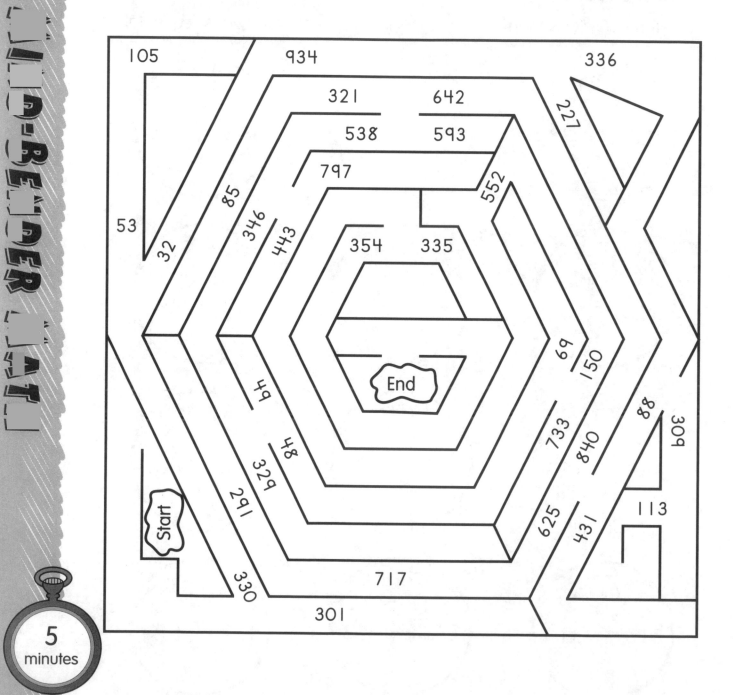

ODD NUMBERS

Activity 64

Directions

Follow the path of odd numbers to reach the end of the maze.

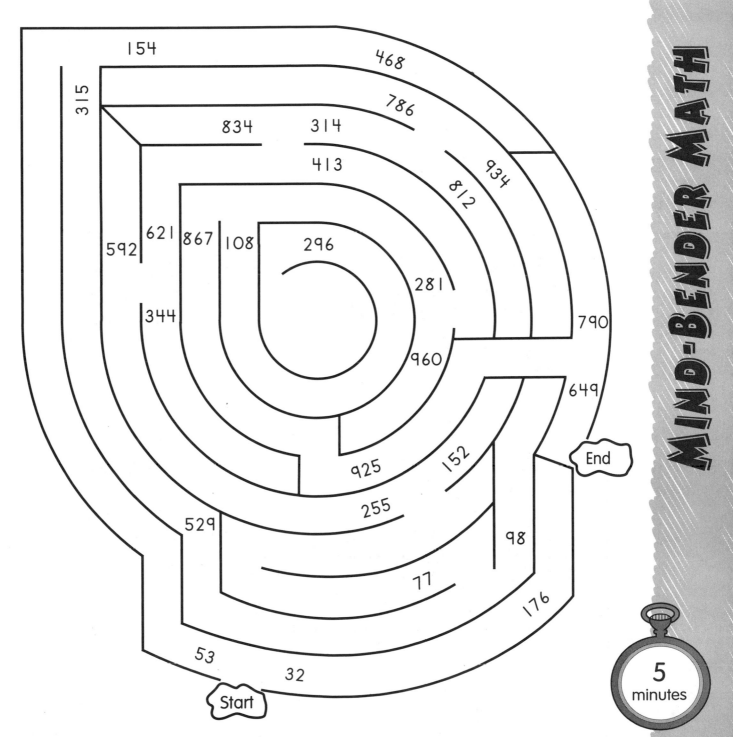

MIND-BENDER MATH

5 minutes

SOLVE IT

Activity 65

Directions

Solve the problems below. Show your work.

1. There were 64 jelly beans in the jar. Now there are only 22 jelly beans. How many jelly beans are missing?

There are _____ jelly beans missing.

4. Mary invited 99 people to the party. Only 30 came. How many people did not come to the party?

_____ people did not come.

2. Jeremy counted 96 stars on Monday and only 26 on Tuesday. How many fewer stars did Jeremy see on Tuesday than on Monday?

Jeremy saw _____ fewer stars on Tuesday.

5. Leo baked 30 cupcakes for his class. His dog ate 20 of the cupcakes. How many cupcakes does Leo have left?

Leo has _____ cupcakes left.

3. Hansel has 75 pieces of candy. He gives 35 pieces to Gretel. How many pieces of candy does Hansel have left?

Hansel has _____ pieces of candy left.

6. Ivan recycled 14 cans of soda and 25 bundles of newspapers. How many items did Ivan recycle in all?

Ivan recycled _____ items in all.

10 minutes

COUNTING MONEY

Directions

Count the money the students found in their pockets.

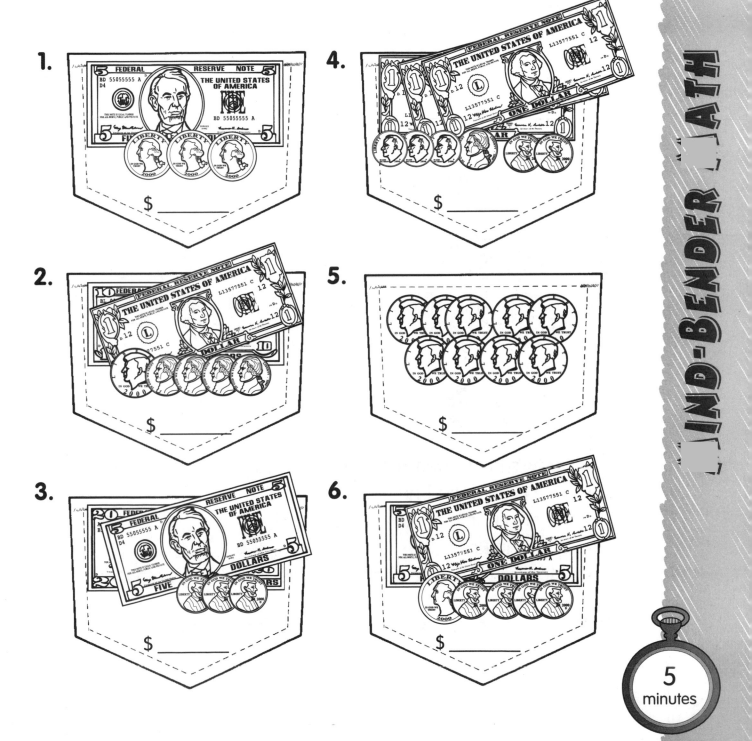

1.

4.

$ _____ $ _____

2.

5.

$ _____ $ _____

3.

6.

$ _____ $ _____

MIND-BENDER MATH

5 minutes

CLASSROOM LOGIC

Activity
67

Directions

Read the clues to discover each student's classroom number. Mark an "O" for yes. Mark an "X" for no.

MIND-BENDER MATH

		2	11	26	37	58
Judy						
Abe						
Marilyn						
Bud						
Carol						

- Judy is in an even-numbered classroom.
- Abe is in an odd-numbered classroom.
- Marilyn is in a higher-numbered classroom than Carol.
- Bud is in Room 37.
- Judy is in a higher-numbered classroom than both Carol and Marilyn.

Write the classroom number next to each student's name.

Judy _____   Abe _____   Marilyn _____   Bud _____   Carol _____

10 minutes

MATH WORDS

Activity
68

Directions

Find and color each math word from the box in the word search below.

A	D	A	P	R	O	D	U	C	T	Q	F
D	I	F	F	E	R	E	N	C	E	U	A
D	G	B	M	O	C	Q	U	S	V	O	C
D	I	V	I	D	E	U	M	U	E	T	T
D	T	E	N	D	F	A	B	B	N	I	O
J	S	L	U	I	O	L	E	T	G	E	R
K	S	M	S	N	N	P	R	R	S	N	T
H	U	N	D	R	E	D	S	A	V	T	T
W	M	X	Y	P	S	A	B	C	C	D	E
T	M	P	O	L	N	M	L	T	E	Y	N
S	R	Q	M	U	L	T	I	P	L	Y	S
T	H	O	U	S	A	N	D	K	J	I	H

MIND-BENDER MATH

add	even	numbers	quotient
difference	factor	odd	subtract
digits	hundreds	ones	sum
divide	minus	plus	tens
equal	multiply	product	thousand

15 minutes

MATH MACHINE 1

Directions

When the professor fed the number ⬚6⬚
into the machine, it came out as ⬚10⬚.
What were the results when he fed in the other numbers?

Example: ⬚6⬚ + 6 = 12 − 2 = ⬚10⬚

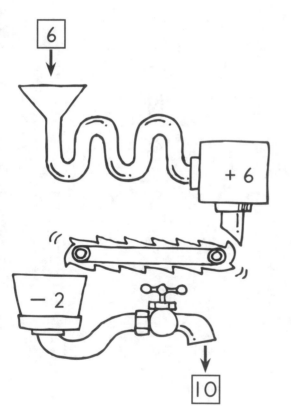

a. 4 _____

b. 10 _____

c. 3 _____

d. 20 _____

e. 12 _____

f. 15 _____

g. 30 _____

h. 18 _____

15 minutes

MATH MACHINE 2

Directions

Here is another professor's math machine. When it was fed 4, it came out as 14. What were the results when she fed in the other numbers?

Example: $4 \times 2 = 8 + 6 = 14$

4

$\times 2$

$+ 6$

14

a. 2 _____

b. 3 _____

c. 5 _____

d. 10 _____

e. 6 _____

f. 7 _____

g. 8 _____

h. 9 _____

INDEPENDENT

15 minutes

LEFT AND RIGHT

Activity
71

Directions

Match each picture on the left with its partner on the right.

BEYOND BRAINY

5 minutes

SHADOW PLAY

Directions

Draw lines to match the shadow picture pairs that go together.

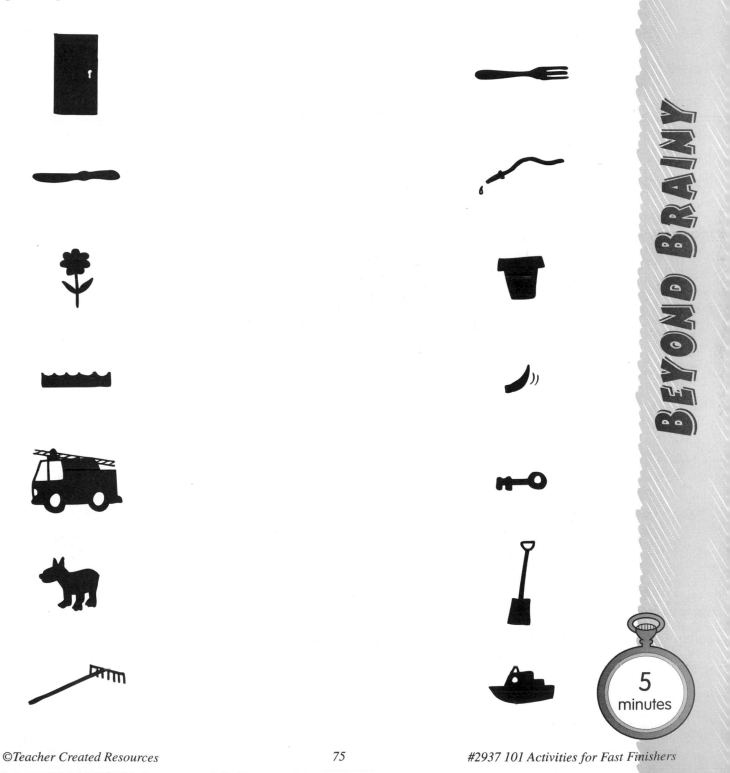

5 minutes

Beyond Brainy

SHAPING THE PUZZLE

Directions

Find the correct shape by reading the clues below.

BEYOND BRAINY

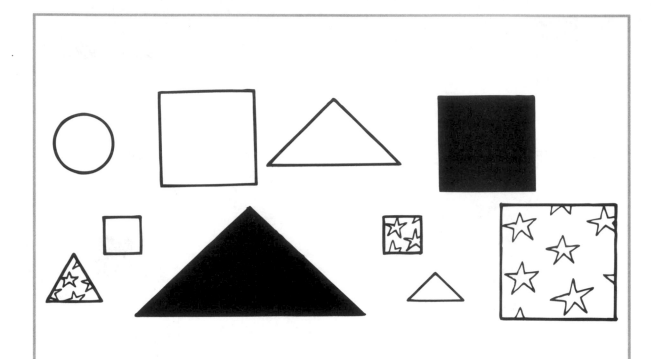

- It does not have stars.
- It is not dark.
- It is smaller than the circle.
- It has only three sides.

Circle the correct shape.

5 minutes

SHAPE COUNT

Activity 74

Directions

Look at the shapes in the picture. Using a different color for each shape, color in the shapes and count how many of each you find. Write your answers on the lines below.

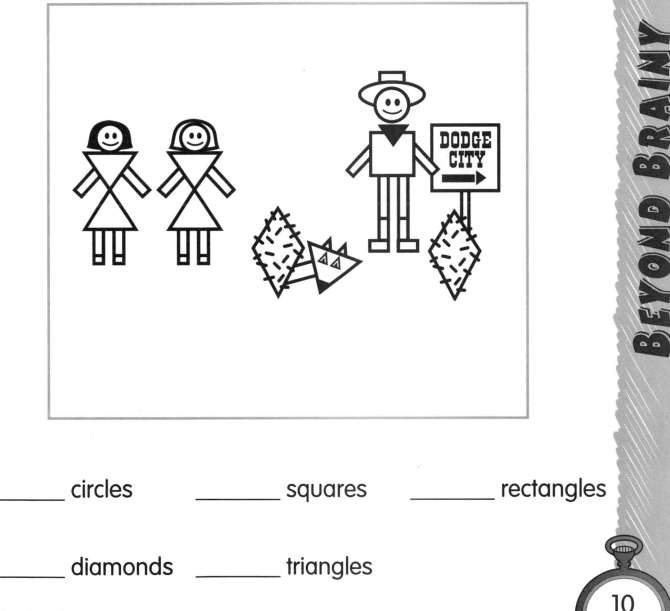

_____ circles   _____ squares   _____ rectangles

_____ diamonds   _____ triangles

Which shape do you see most? _____

Beyond Brainy

10 minutes

WHAT'S MISSING?

Activity
15

Directions

Circle the piece in each box that best completes the shapes so that there are no open lines.

BEYOND BRAINY

1.

2.

3.

4.

5.

6.

5 minutes

TAKE ME HOME

Activity
76

Directions

Draw lines from each animal to its home. Connect the bird to the nest and the ant to the hill. Use a different color for each path.

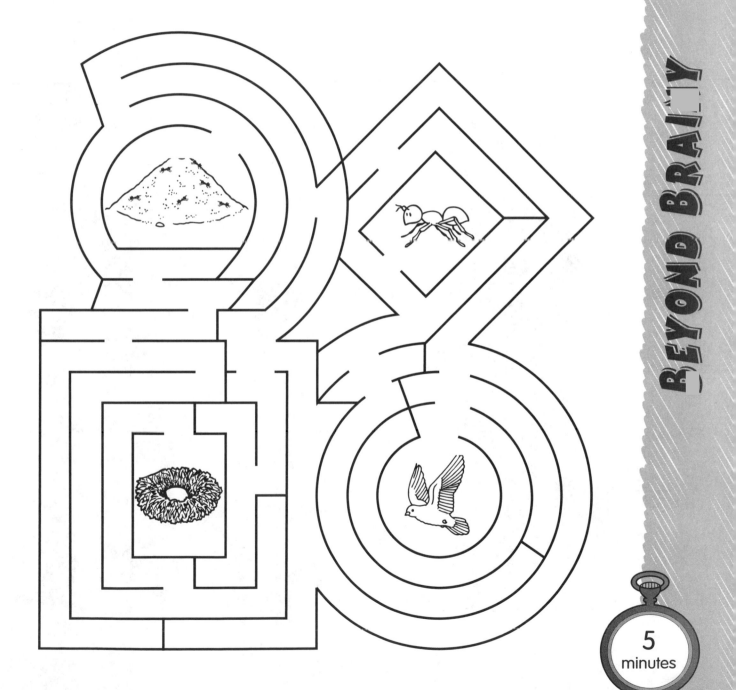

BEYOND BRAINY

5 minutes

ORDER OF EVENTS

Directions

Look at the three pictures in each set. Write *beginning*, *middle*, or *end* under each picture to tell the order of events.

BEYOND BRAIN

1.

_____   _____   _____

2.

_____   _____   _____

3.

_____   _____   _____

5 minutes

PICTURE PUZZLE

Directions

Look closely at the two pictures. In the second one a number of changes have been made. Circle the differences. How many did you find? _____

BEYOND BRAINY

5 minutes

THE MESSY ROOM

Directions

Jason spilled his box of lowercase letters in his messy room. Help Jason find his lowercase letters. Circle or color the ones you find.

BEYOND BRAIN

10 minutes

ITEMS IN A CLASSROOM

Activity 80

Directions

Use the clues below to fill in the puzzle with items you might find in a classroom.

BEYOND BRAINY

Across

5. you cut with it

7. you write with it and erase

8. you fix tears with it

13. you put papers together with it

14. you sit on it

15. you color with them

Down

1. you take this after you study

2. you write on it

3. you read it

4. you find meanings of words with it

6. you use it to search the Internet

9. you type with it

10. you store books in it

11. you sit at it

12. you create a portfolio with it

10 minutes

It's Gone!

Activity

81

Directions

Here are some pictures of family members helping around the home. What is missing in each one? Draw it and then color the pictures.

BEYOND BRAINY

10 minutes

WHAT HAPPENED?

Activity

82

Directions

Look at the pictures on the left. What happened next? Draw a line to match the picture pairs.

1.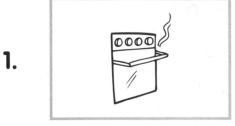

2.

3.

4.

5 minutes

Hidden Animals

Activity
83

Directions

Hidden in each sentence are two or three animal names. Can you find them? Circle them, and write the names on the lines.

Example: Help igloos! → pig

1. It cannot be easy to add. _____

2. Can tall people be archers? _____

3. I was wanting oatmeal. _____

4. Bob ate elves in his dream. _____

5. The hero binds Chief Roger in a billion ropes.

_____

BEYOND BRAINY

10 minutes

SPORT SCRAMBLES

Activity
84

Directions

Unscramble the letters to find the sports.

1. llbseaba _____

2. tblfooal _____

3. bfotslla _____

4. skeblbatal _____

5. ninnrug _____

6. kcyeho _____

7. llorer stngkai _____

8. lngiias _____

9. yccbingli _____

10. inksig _____

11. tbrdingksaeoa _____

12. cei stngkai _____

13. nisnet _____

14. eylvlbaoll _____

15. mnticsgyas _____

BEYOND BRAINY

10 minutes

WHAT'S WRONG?

Activity
85

Directions

Look at this picture carefully. Draw an X over all the things that are wrong. Then draw one more thing that is wrong and one thing that is right.

5 minutes

CIRCLES ALL AROUND

Activity
86

Directions

Count the number of circles you can find in this picture.

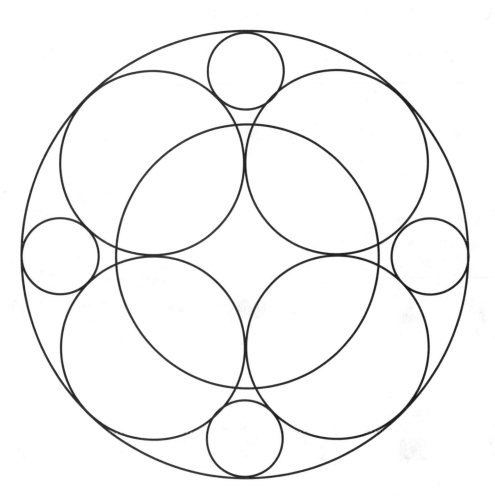

There are _____ circles.

5 minutes

#2937 101 Activities for Fast Finishers

SECRET CODE

Directions

Crack the code to figure out the message.

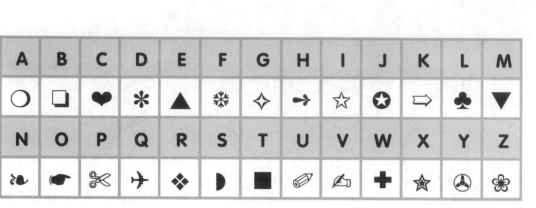

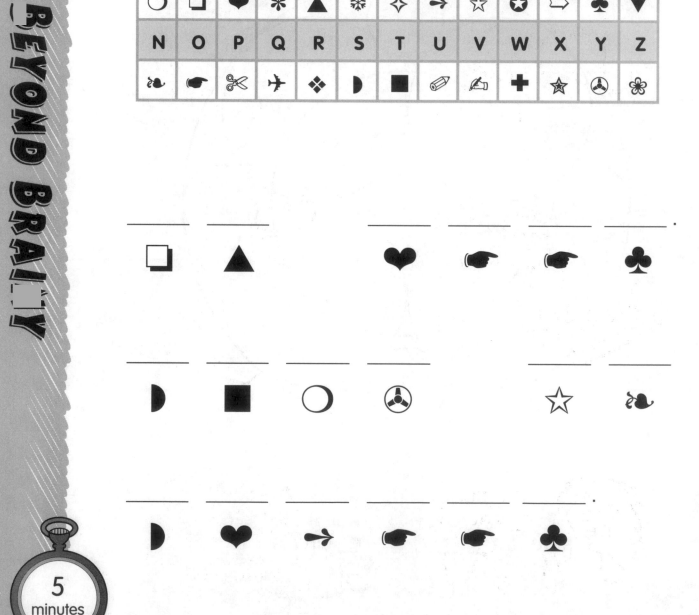

BEYOND BRAINY

5 minutes

SEQUENCING

Activity
88

Directions

In the top-left corner of each box, number the pictures in the order they would happen.

BEYOND BRAIN

5 minutes

CHANGES

Directions

Look how A has changed to B:

A   B

Now look at C:

C

Which shape would C change to in the same way?

The answer is: ★

Now try these patterns. Circle the correct shape in each row.

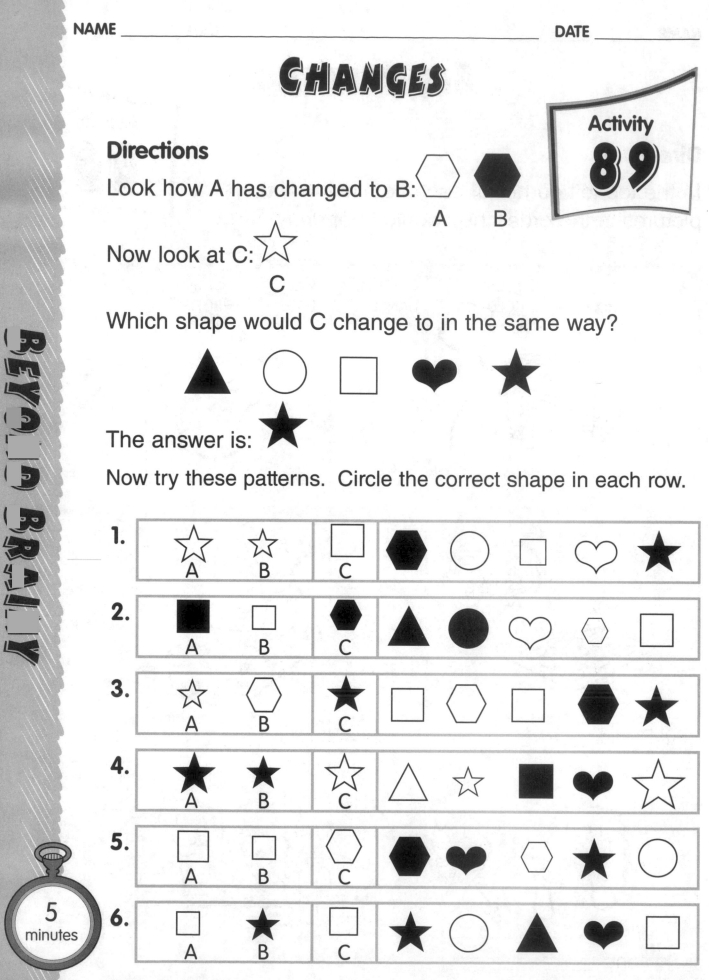

FAMOUS PAIRS

Directions

Use the words in the box to complete the famous pairs below. Then find the words in the word search.

FRIES	MOUSE	DOWN	SEEK	THIN
JELLY	YOUNG	WHITE	RIGHT	STONES
FRONT	COLD	DANCE	EGGS	BUTTER

```
T  D  E  P  V  A  R  G  K  W  M  Y
B  N  X  G  S  W  J  N  I  D  H  R
L  W  O  V  G  O  E  W  A  O  A  I
S  E  I  R  F  S  S  N  H  M  Y  G
Y  Q  G  N  F  E  X  V  U  I  X  H
L  X  Q  D  N  K  E  E  S  G  T  T
L  X  A  O  B  U  T  T  E  R  M  E
E  H  T  W  N  Z  P  K  T  O  C  U
J  S  N  N  I  M  B  H  U  N  O  W
C  C  O  L  D  T  I  S  A  Y  N  V
G  N  U  O  Y  N  E  D  O  U  N  G
```

BREAD and _____

LEFT and _____

UP and _____

STICKS and _____

CAT and _____

OLD and _____

HOT and _____

SONG and _____

BLACK and _____

HAMBURGER and _____

THICK and _____

PEANUT BUTTER and _____

BACK and _____

HIDE and _____

BACON and _____

GOING PLACES

Activity

91

Directions

Follow the directions below to locate the correct vehicle.

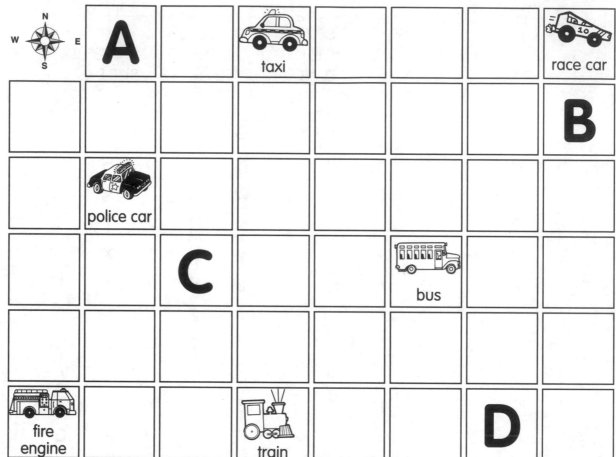

Directions #1

1. Start at A.
2. Go south 3 spaces.
3. Go east 4 spaces.
4. Name the vehicle: _____

Directions #3

1. Start at B.
2. Go north 1 space.
3. Go west 4 spaces.
4. Name the vehicle: _____

Directions #2

1. Start at C.
2. Go south 2 spaces.
3. Go west 2 spaces.
4. Name the vehicle: _____

Directions #4

1. Start at D.
2. Go north 5 spaces.
3. Go east 1 space.
4. Name the vehicle: _____

PET PUZZLER

Activity
92

Directions

Amal's parents gave her a pet for her birthday. Can you tell which pet they gave her? Use the clues below to help you. Then color Amal's pet.

Clues

- It doesn't have fur.
- It doesn't eat meat.
- It cannot fly.

If you could pick a pet for your birthday, what would you pick? Draw it in the box.

BEYOND BRAINY

5 minutes

PEOPLE MOVERS

Beyond Brainy

Directions

People use different modes of transportation to move from place to place every day. Read each set of clues below to help you find out what kind of mover is being described. Write the name and draw a picture for each answer in the boxes.

1. This people mover goes in the sky but does not have wheels.	
2. This one has two large metal pieces that stick out on each side. It also has a row of windows on both sides.	
3. This mover can go fast, but not much faster than 120 miles per hour. It has four wheels.	
4. If you ride in this one, you will not be moving on land, but you might feel the wind in your hair.	
5. This one is best if you use it on dirt or sidewalks. It does not need a motor.	

10 minutes

SPOT THE ERROR

Activity
94

Directions

Find the mistake in each picture. Draw an X over it. Then write what is wrong on the lines below the pictures.

1. _____

_____

BEYOND BRAINY

2. _____

_____

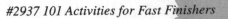

5 minutes

PAT'S LUNCH BOX

Activity 95

Directions

Pat lost his lunch box. Can you help him find it? Circle the correct lunch box. Here are facts about Pat's lunch box.

✔ It has three latches.

✔ It does not have flowers on it.

✔ It has a handle.

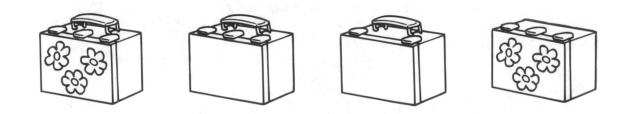

5 minutes

BEYOND BRAINY

WHO WORE WHAT?

Directions

Kevin, Jenna, and Marcus wore hats. Read each clue. Mark the chart to see who wore which hat.

Clues:

✔ Marcus did not wear the baseball cap or the beanie.

✔ Jenna did not wear the beanie.

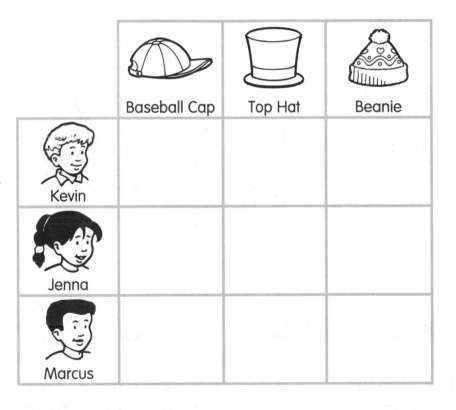

	Baseball Cap	Top Hat	Beanie
Kevin			
Jenna			
Marcus			

1. What kind of hat did Kevin wear? _____

2. What kind of hat did Jenna wear? _____

3. What kind of hat did Marcus wear? _____

5 minutes

BEYOND BRAINY

STARTS WITH "C"

Directions

Use the words in the box and the clues to help fill in the puzzle with words that begin with the letter "c."

BEYOND BRAINY

century	closed
clean	colors
car	cheek
country	church
computer	cat
cold	ceiling
correct	cub

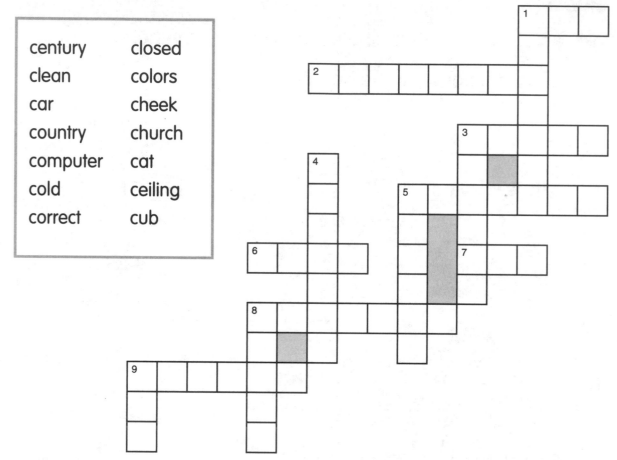

Across

1. what a kitten grows up to be
2. has a keyboard
3. on the side of your face
5. you and millions of others live in one
6. opposite of hot
7. take a ride in it
8. it has 100 years in it
9. not open

Down

1. what you want your answers to be
3. many people go here on Sunday
4. high above you in school or home
5. the rainbow has 7 of these
8. when your clothes are finished washing
9. a baby bear

10 minutes

Before and After

Activity

98

Directions

Complete each sentence with the words *before* or *after*.

1. Eat your dinner _____ you have dessert.

2. You may watch television _____ you do your homework.

3. Clean up the puzzle _____ you take out another toy.

4. New Year's Day is _____ New Year's Eve.

5. We have to turn on the television _____ we can watch the movie.

6. Brush your teeth _____ you go to bed.

7. During the week, Tuesday comes _____ Wednesday.

8. Sometimes you can see a rainbow _____ it rains.

9. February comes _____ the month of January.

10. The letter *m* comes _____ the letter *x*.

11. Most babies learn to crawl _____ they learn to walk.

12. The number 6 comes _____ the number 5.

BEYOND BRAINY

5 minutes

WHAT COINS?

Directions

Color the coins that make the correct amount.

BEYOND BRAINY

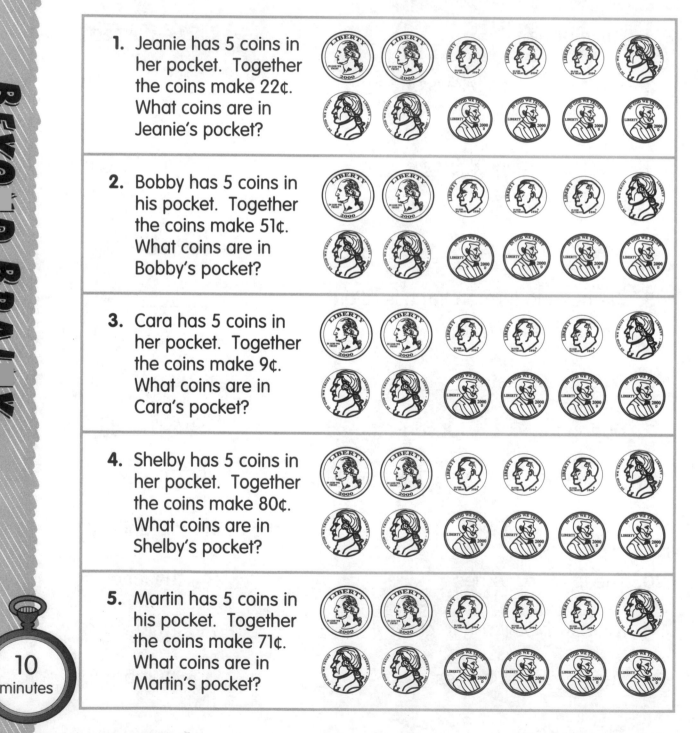

1. Jeanie has 5 coins in her pocket. Together the coins make 22¢. What coins are in Jeanie's pocket?

2. Bobby has 5 coins in his pocket. Together the coins make 51¢. What coins are in Bobby's pocket?

3. Cara has 5 coins in her pocket. Together the coins make 9¢. What coins are in Cara's pocket?

4. Shelby has 5 coins in her pocket. Together the coins make 80¢. What coins are in Shelby's pocket?

5. Martin has 5 coins in his pocket. Together the coins make 71¢. What coins are in Martin's pocket?

10 minutes

LOGIC MAZE

Activity
100

Directions

Move up/down or left/right (not diagonal) to a space that has one of the same symbols as the box you are in.

Example:

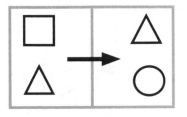

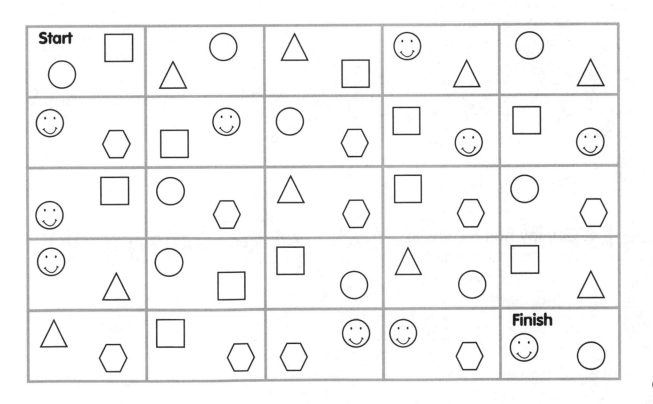

IN THE PAST

Directions

The pictures below show something that was used in the past. In the box beside each one, draw a picture of what we use today instead.

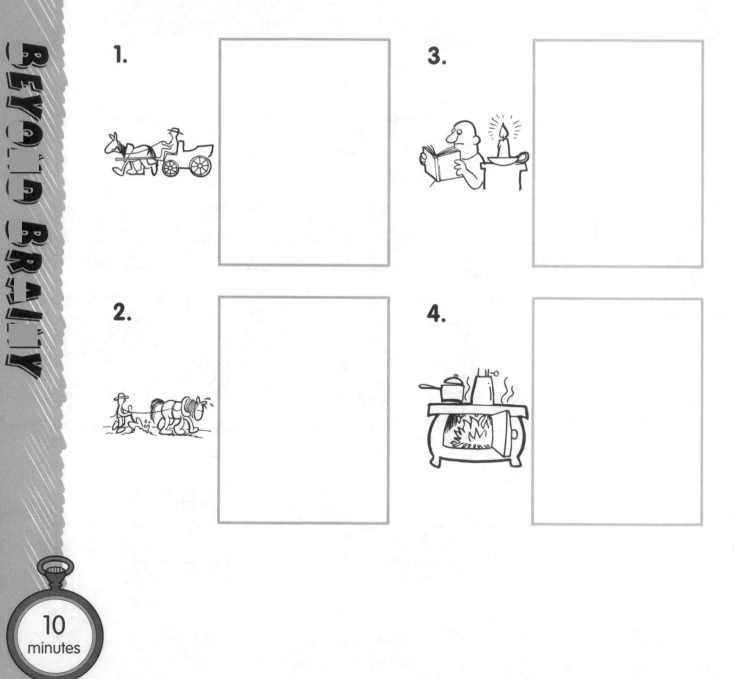

1.

3.

2.

4.

BEYOND BRAINY

10 minutes

ANSWER KEY

Activity 1
1. lamp, palm
2. ship, hips
3. pea, ape
4. star, rats or arts
5. pool, loop or polo
6. saw, was

Activity 2
Possible answers: sand, sea, shells, shovel, snail, sun, sailboat, swimmer, shade, shadow, shower, steps, seats, sandcastle

Activity 3
1. net
2. dog
3. rat
4. tub
5. pin
6. spot
7. step
8. deer

Activity 4
1. crown
2. foot
3. moon
4. sheep
5. ball
6. wood
7. wind
8. card

Activity 5
Red (4 legs): chair, pig, goat, dog, tiger, zebra, cat, table

Yellow (2 legs): girl, boy, goose, lady, hen, owl, duck, man

Activity 6
1. ant
2. car
3. pan or ant
4. hen
5. rat
6. rain

Activity 7
Possible answers: fad, fan, fed, fin, fish, fun, sham, shed, ship, shin, shun, shush, than, them, then, thin, this, thud, thus, wad, wan, was, wash, wed, win, wish, with

Activity 8
A. Across: 1. boat
   Down: 1. bone, 2. tent
B. Across: 2. ship, 3. flag
   Down: 1. hill
C. Across: 1. four, 4. egg
   Down: 2. one, 3. rugs
D. Across: 2. teeth
   Down: 1. tears, 3. train

Activity 9
Answers will vary.

Activity 10
Check drawings for accuracy.

Activity 11
1. pig
2. bed

Activity 12
Things to Eat: cake, eggs, fruit, pizza
Things to Play: tennis, cards, games, football
Things to Wear: shoes, socks, hat, sweater

Activity 13
These boxes should be colored: car, tree, bus, sails, fence, snake, tent, boat, table, fire, water, rocks

Activity 14
1. car, star, scar
2. fancy, Nancy, antsy
3. solar, polar, molar
4. hairy, fairy, Jerry
5. calf, laugh, half
6. head, bed, fed
7. cake, rake, shake
8. pipe, stripe, type
9–11. Answers will vary.

Activity 15
Jack and Jill went up the hill

Rub-a-dub-dub three men in a tub

Wee Willie Winkie runs through the town

Little Boy Blue come blow your horn

Humpty Dumpty sat on a wall

Little Bo Peep has lost her sheep

ANSWER KEY (cont.)

Activity 16
Person nouns (red): brother, child, nurse, sister, teacher
Place nouns (yellow): bedroom, circus, hospital, school, store
Thing nouns (blue): book, car, crayons, desk, rainbow

Activity 17
People verbs (red): skip, cook, ski, sing, drive, shoot, talk, whisper, skate, roller blade, speak, yell, dress, read, write
Animal verbs (blue): quack, fly, bark, hiss, gallop, trot, chirp
People and Animal verbs (green): run, jump, grow, turn, roll, push, swim, eat, scratch, bite, play, drink, sit, gulp, hop, throw, fall, whistle, swallow, lay, sleep, walk, think

Activity 18
How Many?: million dollars, six boys, a dozen eggs, one teacher
What Kind?: short hair, rich man, hot cement, green shoes
Which One?: these books, that bus, this computer, any class

Activity 19
1. tree
2. kitten
3. apple pie
4. skateboard
5. bed
6. shoes
7. fire
8. sky

Activity 20
1. yes
2. no
3. no
4. yes
5. yes
6. yes

Activity 21
bathrobe, necklace, overalls, raincoat, shoelace, swimsuit, turtleneck, wristwatch

Activity 22
Answers may vary.
Possible answers include:
1. house
2. tree
3. bicycle
4. bird

Activity 23
1. hill
2. water
3. crown
4. after
5. lamb
6. snow
7. went
8. go

Activity 24
List A
1. cake
2. candy
3. caramel
4. chocolate
5. cookies
List B
1. panther
2. parrot
3. pelican
4. penguin
5. puppy
List C
1. Alex
2. Alicia
3. Allison
4. Amanda
5. Ann

Activity 25
Answers may vary.
Possible answers include:
1. ghost
2. ox
3. mouse
4. bird
5. wink
6. fox
7. night
8. whip
9. snail
10. kitten

Activity 26

box: a cube-shaped container; to play a sport that allows hitting

bowl: to play a sport with balls and pins; a round, deep dish

can: to be able to; a metal or aluminum container

ear: something to hear with; a corn cob

foot: a lower body part; twelve inches in length

pupil: a student; the inner part of one's eye

shower: a light rain; used to clean oneself

staple: metal to fasten papers together; a standard food item

tie: to fasten items together; an item worn around a man's neck

wave: moving a hand back and forth; the cresting water in the ocean

Activity 27

1st sentence: duck, pond, dog, cat
2nd sentence: duck, nest
3rd sentence: nest, eggs
4th sentence: snake, hole, duck

Activity 28

1. lemon
2. wool
3. garden
4. pencil
5. tiger
6. bucket

Activity 29

1. day
2. dark/heavy
3. cold
4. beautiful/pretty
5. sad
6. soft/easy
7. bad
8. top

Activity 30

1. bare: without a cover
   bear: a big, furry animal
2. dear: a greeting in a letter
   deer: a forest animal
3. brake: to stop
   break: to smash
4. close: to shut
   clothes: what you wear
5. grate: shred into pieces
   great: very good
6. sent: did send
   scent: a smell

Activity 31

1. ?   5. .
2. !   6. .
3. .   7. !
4. ?   8. .

Activity 32

1. Is today your birthday?
2. A party is a wonderful idea!
3. Mike will bring the birthday cake.
4. How many candles will be on the cake?
5. Will there be a clown?
6. We can help you decorate.
7. Karen will bring the balloons.
8. The party will have lots of music.
9. There will be many presents.
10. What a wonderful birthday it will be!

Activity 33

1. clown
2. a cat
3. pizza
4. circle

Activity 34

Answers will vary.

Activity 35

Answers will vary.

Activity 36

Toni's balloons (red):
    8, 12, 16, 18
Sally's balloons (yellow):
    5, 9, 17, 19
Mika's balloons (blue):
    21, 25, 33, 100

Activity 37

8	3	2	0	4	8	40	3	99	21
5	9	7	4	11	48	21	6	8	14
11	12	13	6	46	9	12	9	7	11
3	6	41	8	44	7	15	3	6	9
7	9	10	21	16	42	18	21	9	8
16	14	12	22	13	40	7	24	27	48
18	12	11	23	36	38	6	7	30	45
20	13	20	5	34	6	5	9	33	42
14	22	24	7	32	5	8	8	36	39
15	18	26	28	30	4	3	11	6	7
16	17	19	9	11	0	11	4	5	6

Activity 38

Possible answers:

$6 + 2 = 8$

$2 + 6 = 8$

$4 \times 2 = 8$

$2 \times 4 = 8$

$10 - 2 = 8$

$5 + 3 = 8$

$3 + 5 = 8$

$7 + 1 = 8$

$1 + 7 = 8$

$4 + 1 + 3 = 8$

$5 + 1 + 2 = 8$

$6 + 3 - 1 = 8$

$7 + 2 - 1 = 8$

$4 + 5 - 1 = 8$

Activity 39

Row 1: 10, 9, 8, 10, 9

Row 2: 20, 12, 4, 14, 12

Row 3: 6, 4, 20, 6, 8

Row 4: 9, 9, 12, 20, 14

Row 5: 8, 10, 4, 6, 14

Appears four times = 9

Activity 40

There are 19 triangles.

Activity 41

Colored puppies: 12, 6, 18, 24, 20, 16

Even numbers: 2, 4, 6, 8, 10, 12, 14, 16, 18, 20, 22, 24

Activity 42

cone: 8

cube: 1

circle: 6

cylinder: 9

rectangle: 6

Answer: cylinder

Activity 43

1. Ben
2. Jacinta
3. Sally
4. Hamid

Activity 44

Zoe: 3 kites;

$6 + 6, 8 + 4, 10 + 2$

Jodi: 4 kites;

$7 + 2, 5 + 4, 6 + 3, 3 \times 3$

Tim: 3 kites;

$10 \times 2, 10 + 10, 18 + 2$

Meg: 4 kites;

$6 + 4, 5 \times 2, 5 + 5, 12 - 2$

Activity 45

Activity 46

1. 6
2. 5
3. 8
4. 9
5. 10
6. 14
7. 11

Answer: computer

Activity 47

1. 12
2. 1
3. 16
4. 20
5. 15
6. 14

Activity 48

$2 + 4 = 11 - 5$

$4 + 3 = 13 - 6$

$6 + 2 = 11 - 3$

$4 + 7 = 16 - 5$

$3 + 9 = 19 - 7$

$6 + 8 = 22 - 8$

$5 + 10 = 15 - 0$

$6 + 3 = 14 - 5$

$3 + 7 = 14 - 4$

$7 + 9 = 20 - 4$

$4 + 1 = 17 - 12$

$4 + 9 = 17 - 4$

$11 + 6 = 21 - 4$

$9 + 9 = 19 - 1$

Activity 49

Across

1. 4,958
2. 7,352
5. 3,839
7. 8,786
8. 5,187
10. 4,018
11. 7,951

Down

1. 4,134
3. 5,865
4. 7,647
6. 9,810
9. 1,251

Activity 50

15 + 5 and 10 + 10 = 20
6 x 2 and 6 + 6 = 12
4 x 2 and 4 + 4 = 8
5 + 5 and 6 + 4 = 10

Activity 51

1. 71
2. 43
3. 86
4. 60
5. 67
6. 81
7. 62

The bull's eye (#4) should be colored green.

Activity 52

orange

Activity 53

1. 15
2. 20
3. 10
4. 16
5. 20
6. 10
7. 16
8. 20
9. 12
10. 10
11. 15
12. 20
13. 12
14. 15
15. 30

Activity 54

1. reading
2. 6
3. science, P.E.
4. math
5. 2

Activity 55

There are 6 squares.

Activity 56

donkey

Activity 57

1. 4
2. 30
3. 9
4. 12
5. 12
6. 25

Activity 58

a crocodile

Activity 59

2 x 5 and 6 + 4 and 20 − 10 = 10
2 x 4 and 5 + 3 and 10 − 2 = 8
7 + 5 and 6 + 6 and 15 − 3 = 12
2 x 7 and 8 + 6 and 9 + 5 = 14

Activity 60

1. 19 + 16 = 35
2. 19 + 37 = 56
3. 45 + 19 = 64
4. 26 + 14 = 40
5. 37 + 26 = 63
6. 45 + 16 = 61
7. 45 + 24 = 69
8. 26 + 18 = 44
9. 18 + 24 = 42

Activity 61

Matthew: 12
Paul: 8
Janet: 14
Sula: 6
Mike: 10

Activity 62

1. >
2. <
3. =
4. <
5. <
6. >
7. <
8. =
9. >
10. >
11. <
12. >

ANSWER KEY (cont.)

Activity 63

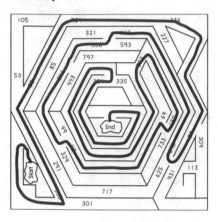

Activity 64

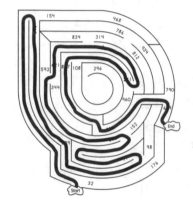

Activity 65
1. 42
2. 70
3. 40
4. 69
5. 10
6. 39

Activity 66
1. $5.75
2. $11.70
3. $25.03
4. $3.37
5. $4.50
6. $6.29

Activity 67
Judy: 58
Abe: 11
Marilyn: 26
Bud: 37
Carol: 2

Activity 68
(word search grid)

Activity 69
a. 4 + 6 = 10 − 2 = 8
b. 10 + 6 = 16 − 2 = 14
c. 3 + 6 = 9 − 2 = 7
d. 20 + 6 = 26 − 2 = 24
e. 12 + 6 = 18 − 2 = 16
f. 15 + 6 = 21 − 2 = 19
g. 30 + 6 = 36 − 2 = 34
h. 18 + 6 = 24 − 2 = 22

Activity 70
a. 2 x 2 = 4 + 6 = 10
b. 3 x 2 = 6 + 6 = 12
c. 5 x 2 = 10 + 6 = 16
d. 10 x 2 = 20 + 6 = 26
e. 6 x 2 = 12 + 6 = 18
f. 7 x 2 = 14 + 6 = 20
g. 8 x 2 = 16 + 6 = 22
h. 9 x 2 = 18 + 6 = 24

Activity 71
1. bone
2. carrot
3. net
4. mouse
5. sock
6. cheese

Activity 72
door—key
knife—fork
flower—pot
water—boat
fire truck—hose
dog—tail
rake—shovel

Activity 73
The small, white triangle should be circled.

Activity 74
circles: 3
squares: 6
rectangles: 20
diamonds: 2
triangles: 14
Answer: rectangles

Activity 75
1. first piece
2. fourth piece
3. second piece
4. second piece
5. first piece
6. third piece

Activity 76

Activity 77

1. middle, beginning, end
2. beginning, end, middle
3. beginning, end, middle

Activity 78

10 differences: person on the left's hair, eyes, holding a shovel, no flag on sandcastle, top edge of sandcastle, windows on sandcastle, girl's hat, bathing suit, necklace, rocks at bottom

Activity 79

All 26 letters are included in the picture. Check page for accuracy.

Activity 80

Across
   5. scissors
   7. pencil
   8. tape
   13. stapler
   14. chair
   15. crayons

Down
   1. test
   2. paper
   3. book
   4. dictionary
   6. computer
   9. keyboard
   10. bookcase
   11. desk
   12. folder

Activity 81

1. lawnmower
2. broom
3. paintbrush
4. hedge clippers

Activity 82

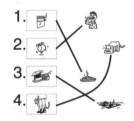

Activity 83

1. bee, toad
2. ant, bear
3. swan, ant, goat
4. bat, eel
5. robin, frog, lion

Activity 84

1. baseball
2. football
3. softball
4. basketball
5. running
6. hockey
7. roller skating
8. sailing
9. bicycling
10. skiing
11. skateboarding
12. ice skating
13. tennis
14. volleyball
15. gymnastics

Activity 85

Check page for accuracy.

Activity 86

There are 10 circles.

Activity 87

Message: Be cool. Stay in school.

Activity 88

ANSWER KEY (cont.)

Activity 89
1. small square
2. small hexagon
3. black hexagon
4. small, white star
5. small, white hexagon
6. black star

Activity 90
bread and butter
left and right
up and down
sticks and stones
cat and mouse
old and young
hot and cold
song and dance
black and white
hamburger and fries
thick and thin
peanut butter and jelly
back and front
hide and seek
bacon and eggs

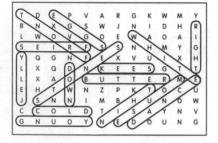

Activity 91
1. bus
2. fire engine
3. taxi
4. race car

Activity 92
Amal's pet = fish

Activity 93
1. helicopter
2. airplane
3. car
4. boat
5. bicycle

Activity 94
1. The TV is not plugged in.
2. The dust should be behind the horses.

Activity 95
Pat's lunch box has three latches, no flowers, and a handle.

Activity 96
1. Kevin = beanie
2. Jenna = baseball cap
3. Marcus = top hat

Activity 97

Across
1. cat
2. computer
3. cheek
5. country
6. cold
7. car
8. century
9. closed

Down
1. correct
3. church
4. ceiling
5. colors
8. clean
9. cub

Activity 98
Answers may vary.
1. before
2. after
3. before
4. after
5. before
6. before
7. before
8. after
9. after
10. before
11. before
12. after

Activity 99
1. 1 dime, 2 nickels, 2 pennies
2. 1 quarter, 2 dimes, 1 nickel, 1 penny
3. 1 nickel, 4 pennies
4. 2 quarters, 3 dimes
5. 2 quarters, 2 dimes, 1 penny

Activity 100

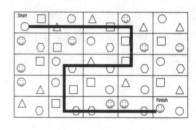

Activity 101
Answers will vary.